A Prostitute

No Longer:

The Devotional

Rev. Lisa R. Pate

Dedication

This book is dedicated to Cornelius (Cornel), April, Israel, Caleb &
my grandchildren, Mylessa Anne & Riley Owen

Thank you to my heartbeat, my firstborn son, Cornel. The day I left you with a crack pipe in my hand, I died. Yet you loved me past my hurt, guilt, and shame. God heard the longing in our hearts for one another and brought us back together; I truly treasure the joys that we now share as a family together. You are now 38 years old. You have granted me access back into your life and into your heart, and for that, I am eternally grateful! To your beautiful wife April, God's chosen vessel for you, my granddaughter Mylessa Ann, and our youngest heart's prayer, Riley Owen, you all are the light in my lamp.

To the two wonders in my world, Israel and Caleb – you both are like air and water to me. I need you both to live. When I wanted to crawl inside of my box filled with mistakes, rejection, and regret, your care pulled me out of that box and made me live and move, to grow from striving to surviving and finally to thriving! You and your love for me have proven and shown me God's true forgiveness and the ability to start life over and live again.

Insight and Encouragement

I have discovered the fascinating and insightful impartation of reading different versions of the Word of God, specifically regarding Scriptures that speak to me. I try to "milk" the Scriptures by reading and receiving the different translations that encourage my heart to search, mine, and excavate (as though searching for gold because I am) every word within the Scriptures that are highlighted to me. It's as though the words Holy Spirit wants me to focus on leap off the page. As I have heard others say, it's like the Holy Spirit gets out a heavenly highlighter and highlights words and phrases so that your attention is drawn there. In those words and phrases, He begins to open up and impart revelation. The more we mine and excavate the Scriptures, the more gold we discover. This is not a physical gold, however; it's so much more! I believe that it is Holy Spirit's desire that we walk through the Scriptures allowing Him to reveal, inspire, encourage, and provide insight and hope that are buried deep within every jot and tittle of the Word of God. We only need to mine the Scriptures for them.

This devotional is written with a 9-week time frame in mind; however, please do not be limited to this time frame. It is my vision that by the time you have completed this devotional, you will be well on your way to a life transformed by the power of the Holy Spirit in Jesus' name. As you will notice, instead of chapters, this devotional is written and introduced in layers and originally designed to work alongside my book, *A Prostitute No Longer*. It is my experience that the traumas that you and I have faced have been layered upon us by the enemy of our souls. Upon reading, receiving, and partaking in the deliverance that is imparted in each layer, you will be made free as each layer is lifted from your life and burned up by the fire of God. As you read, participate in, and meditate upon the writings within this devotional, I pray that the robe of God's righteousness will cover you and the peace of God will surround you in Jesus' name.

I encourage you not to rush the process. This devotional is a journey. Every day is not written as a typical devotional with a paragraph and a thought. This devotional is written to encourage one to spend time in the presence of the Lord to reveal and expose one's true, deep issues of the heart, thereby bringing healing through the Word of God and the presence of the Holy Spirit. Most devotional layers are prepared with a part for you as the reader to play and participate in; others are times of meditation upon the writings. Therefore, if the Holy Spirit compels you to stay in Layer One – Day One, remain there. Do not rush your process. Our Father is the Almighty Breasted One; draw much needed nourishment from Him and remain in His presence. The longer you remain, the more you will be changed. You are invited to search, dig, and discover all that our Heavenly Father desires to impart. **Receive Him!**

Table of Contents

Layer One ~ Daddy, Keep Silent

Layer One ~ Introduction

Daddy, Keep Silent

The story of my life began as my father was killed because he would not keep silent about me as his daughter. I have come to believe that to keep silent about one's responsibility, place, stature, or child is the utmost rejection; however, our heavenly Father never chose this way for us. In fact, from Genesis to Revelation, He calls out to us, drawing us to His Son, Jesus Christ. One of the most beautiful passages of Scripture is Isaiah 43:1, which says, "But now, thus says the LORD, who created you, O Jacob, And He who formed you, O Israel: 'Fear not, for I have redeemed you; I have called you by your name; You are Mine.'"

Throughout my life as a young believer in Christ, from being newly saved to this present day, this Scripture permeates my spirit with inspired hope. Our heavenly Father, the one who created us, calls us by name, encourages us, and rises to every occasion to acknowledge us as His son or daughter, His friend, and His chosen vessel. He will not be silent about me, and neither will He be silent about you.

Layer One ~ Day One

Daddy, Keep Silent

Isaiah 43:1
"But now, thus says the LORD, who created you, O Jacob, And He who formed you, O Israel: 'Fear not, for I have redeemed you; I have called you by your name; You are Mine.'"

~Heart Caption~

One of the most effective tools the enemy uses against Christians is our past. He attacks our minds with memories, secret lies, hidden wishes, what ifs, whys, could haves, should haves, would haves, and the questions of how, when, where, and why not. One of the best tools we as Christians have in our arsenal is the Word of God! This was the weapon Jesus used in doing battle against Satan. With this weapon, we are to cast down every thought, take them captive, and render the enemy's lies ineffective by the Word of God. Therefore, it is imperative that we take the Word of God, refresh our spirit, and renew our minds. How do we do this? One of the ways that we can do this is by Scripture reading and memorization. Scripture memorization can change our life and transform our spirit.

Isaiah 43:1 is written above. As you read, memorize, and meditate upon this verse, allow it to penetrate your heart. After reading the Scripture, taking it all in, and then memorizing it, write from memory your heart's prayer regarding Isaiah 43:1.

~Focus Point~

Isaiah 43:1

"But now, thus says the LORD, who created you, O Jacob, And He who formed you, O Israel: 'Fear not, for I have redeemed you; I have called you by your name; You are Mine.'"

My summary of Isaiah 43:1 (what the Scripture is saying to me):

_____

_____

_____

_____

_____

_____

My prayer regarding Isaiah 43:1:

_____

_____

_____

_____

_____

_____

Layer One ~ Day Two

Daddy, Keep Silent

Isaiah 43:1
*"**But now, thus says the LORD,** who created you, O Jacob, And He who formed you, O Israel: 'Fear not, for I have redeemed you; I have called you by your name; You are Mine.'"*

~Heart Caption~

Do you remember your mom or your dad saying to you, "Come here, now!" or "Do what I said, now!"? Hearing the word "now" can be demanding, depending on who is saying it. But listen to the word "now" from a compassionate and loving Father. He says to all His children, "You have gone through a lot. You have experienced a lot of hurt and devastation. But ***now,*** hear what I the Sovereign Lord says about all that you have gone through and how I will use it. I will use all of it, the good, the bad, and the indifferent for good to those who love God, to those who are the called according to My purpose."

Isaiah 43:1
*"**But now, thus says the LORD**, who created you, O Jacob, And He who formed you, O Israel: 'Fear not, for I have redeemed you; I have called you by your name; You are Mine.'"*

<u>Precious one, God is talking to you; He is talking with you NOW.</u>

No matter what you have gone through, stop and observe your NOW. You really are in a different place, and you are not to move forward in the usual manner. Things are different because God is with you, and He is ordering your steps. Now He guides you. Now He leads you. Now He speaks. Now He whispers to you. Hear His gentle voice speaking to you now. Things are changing now. You are seeing things as they are. The unveiling is manifesting, and you are hearing clearly and seeing clearly now.

~Focus Point~

Your experience with God is now. What is your Heavenly Father saying to you about your now? Take a moment and write your experience.

_____

_____

_____

_____

Layer One ~ Day Three

Daddy, Keep Silent

Isaiah 43:1
*"But now, thus says the LORD, **who created you, O Jacob**, And He who formed you, O Israel: 'Fear not, for I have redeemed you; I have called you by your name; You are Mine.'"*

~Heart Caption~

Your heavenly Father has created you. He sent His Son to die for you. To keep silent about you would have been a crime. He is not embarrassed by you nor your sin. Your heavenly Father is not ashamed to call you daughter nor son.

Precious one, you were created by God

I heard it said by a worship leader during a worship event that "Many of us have settled into identities and names that are way, **way** beneath what God has created us to be and what God has in store for us."

Genesis 1:26 says, *"Then God said, 'Let Us make man in Our image, according to Our likeness; let them have dominion over the fish of the sea, over the birds of the air, over the cattle, over all the earth and over every creeping thing that creeps.'"*

In Genesis we read, accept, and believe the word that says: "And God said." From creation all the way to where it references 'every creeping thing,' we believe that God put it all in place. Yet life has dulled our ears to hear, our eyes to see, and our hearts to believe and accept those words as they pertain to **_us_**. *"Then God said, 'let us make man in Our image, according to Our likeness.'"*

We are made in the expressed image of God, our Father, His Son, and the Holy Spirit. Father God is on His throne, Jesus the Christ is seated at His right hand interceding for you, me, and the people of God, Jesus' bride. Beloved, you were made in the image and likeness of your heavenly Father, from the foundation of the earth.

The other portion of that verse says, "Let **_them_** have dominion." Beloved, you were in the mind of God before He awakened Adam to the fact that it was not good for him to be alone and that He would create a help mate for him. Let **_them_** have dominion on the earth was a charge – the measure of authority given from the foundation of the earth. God has not taken it back. Let **_them_** have dominion (complete authority) over the fish, as fish do not rule over humanity. Let **_them_** have dominion over the birds of the air. Birds fly; birds cannot walk upright like a man. Let **_them_** have dominion over the cattle. Cattle walk on four hooves; cattle do not walk upright, they do not talk, and most are only measured for the meat that can be used from them or the leather they produce, yet they have their own beauty. Let **_them_** have dominion over every creeping thing that creeps on the earth.

We have dominion over all the aforementioned animals because we walk upright, speak, have authority to decree and declare, and were made in the image and likeness of our heavenly Father. No other creation on the planet has that ability. All other creatures are not made in the image and likeness of our heavenly Father, except His prized possession, known as humanity – man and woman.

I encourage you to read Genesis chapters 1 and 2 before you move forward to Layer one ~ Day Four. Be encouraged as you review how your heavenly Father created His creation, especially to see your place in it. All of creation was formed by the spoken word of God, but you, beloved, were formed with the finger of God, in His own likeness and in His own image. No other creation on planet earth was created in this manner. You are His chosen possession.

~Focus Point~

Heavenly Father, thank you for creating me in Your image and in Your likeness. Thank you, Father, for giving me dominion over the earth and everything in it. Lord, I am learning, memorizing, and breathing in Your Word which I accept, believe, and apply in and over my life from this day forward so that I can take hold of the authority that is rightfully mine. Lord, Your Word tells me in James 1:22, *"But be a doer of the word, and not hearers only, deceiving yourselves."* Father, in accepting, believing, and applying Your Word, I walk as Your son or daughter in all the rights and privileges Your Word says that I have. Father, I commit to search Your Word for all the promises You have made available to me so that I can know and honor the covenant Your Son died to give me. In Christ's name, amen!

What would you like to write/express to your Father regarding being created in His image?

_____

_____

_____

_____

Layer One ~ Day Four

Daddy, Keep Silent

Isaiah 43:1
*"But now, thus says the LORD, who created you, O Jacob, And **He who formed you**, O Israel: 'Fear not, for I have redeemed you; I have called you by your name; You are Mine.'"*

~Heart Caption~

We are the only creation of God that is made in His image and in His likeness. The Word of God says in Genesis 2:7, *"And the Lord God formed man of the dust of the ground, and breathed into his nostrils the breath of life; and man became a living being."* Every other creation was created merely by the words, decree, declaration, and command of God. Because we were made in His likeness and His image, we are the only created being who bears the *ruach* (breath) of God.

He who formed you

Merriam-Webster defines the word form or formed as the shape and structure of something as distinguished from its material, or a body (as of a person) especially in its external appearance or as distinguished from the face.

~Focus Point~

Beloved, some may often think that since we learned to walk, ride a bicycle, learned 6th grade math, and graduated from school, some may feel that they have pulled themselves up by their own bootstraps. While all these accomplishments are great, you did not form yourself. You did not form your life. You did not form or plan the purpose and destiny for your life.

Before God planned your purpose and destiny, He formed you. Everything that you were ever called to do was formed within you when He formed you: your passions, your gifts, your callings, your hips, your hair texture, your ears, the shape of your nose, your eyes your lips, the size of your heart, and down to the size of your shoe. You were formed by Almighty God! He did not ask anyone else to form you. He did it Himself!

Jeremiah 1:5 says, *"Before I formed you in the womb I knew you; Before you were born I sanctified you; I ordained you a prophet to the nations."* Beautiful one, God formed you; He formed YOU! You may look like your beautiful mom, but God formed you. You may sound like your handsome father, but God formed you. No longer be critical of the beautiful person you are.

Write down some of the beautiful ways you realize, all the more, that your heavenly Father has formed you, beautifully or handsomely.

_____

_____

_____

_____

Layer One ~ Day Five

Daddy, Keep Silent

Isaiah 43:1
*"But now, thus says the LORD, who created you, O Jacob, And He who formed you, O Israel: '**Fear not**, for I have redeemed you; I have called you by your name; You are Mine.'"*

~Heart Caption~

FEAR. We have seen this word written in many ways and interpreted in just as many. One of those ways that we have seen this word is: *False Evidence Appears Real*. But why do we fear? We fear that which we do not know or understand. But Isaiah 43:1 says, **"Fear not."** We hold back from taking kingdom steps because of fear. We lag behind in obedience because of fear. We hesitate and procrastinate because of fear. The very root of procrastination is **fear**.

I have discovered that the phrase *fear not* is written within Scripture more than 150 times from Genesis 20:11 to Revelation 15:4. Other forms of this phrase are also used, such as "do not be afraid" or "do not be anxious." Placed in the proper context of the Scripture of Isaiah 43:1, the people of Israel had every reason to fear. They were facing the Babylonian army and exile. We are facing the COVID-19 virus in the world at the time of this writing, and fear has permeated the media and the airwaves of our world so much so that you can tangibly feel it. We see it with every look outside of the window, every switch of the channel to a movie to avoid the news, only to listen to it on our phones or via social media. However, God reminds us to *fear not*. This is actually a command; it is not a suggestion. God is commanding us to remember Him, His covenant of love, and His banner of protection over us. Remember that we are surrounded and cocooned in His presence and His love. His Word is a shield about us; beloved, *fear not*. The evidence of the situations we are facing and have faced are real, and we can have the courage to face them, even though they may be extremely painful. Christ gives us the fortitude and courage to stand up to the problems, with Him and in Him. His Word is Truth, and when He says to us, "Fear not," He does so realizing that we may be very afraid, yet we are *not alone*. He and His Word are one! Fear not, beloved, for we are covered and wrapped in the love of Jesus Christ.

~Focus Point~

Every warrior has within his or her arsenal arrows that they use when they come up against a giant, or a mountainous situation that is hindering them from moving forward. The arrows are to prohibit what is prohibiting them. The arrows are to annihilate what is trying to annihilate them. Some of the arrows in my arsenal are Scriptures dealing with fear. Below, I give you three Scriptures for you to add to your arsenal.

~Focus Point~

Deuteronomy 31:6
"Be strong and of good courage, do not fear nor be afraid of them;
for the LORD your God, He is the One who goes with you.
He will not leave you nor forsake you."

Isaiah 41:10
"Fear not, for I am with you;
Be not dismayed, for I am your God.

I will strengthen you, Yes, I will help you,
I will uphold you with My Righteous right hand."

Psalm 56:3
"Whenever I am afraid, I will trust in You."

What are some situations or circumstances that you have fought through? What are some things that others have said that have crept into your life, mind, or heart that have caused you to be fearful?

_____

_____

_____

_____

     Now that you have confessed the situations or circumstances out loud by writing them down, as an act of faith, take authority over them and write out your prayer to God of how you will no longer allow fear to hijack your mind, hands, or heart and cause you to stop, procrastinate, and become immobile regarding the things and the directives of God.

Father, in Jesus' name and by the power of the Holy Spirit, I will no longer be fearful about...

_____

_____

_____

_____

But I will stand in Your love, in Your strength, and in Your mighty power.

Layer One ~ Day Six

Daddy, Keep Silent

Isaiah 43:1
*"But now, thus says the LORD, who created you, O Jacob, And He who formed you, O Israel: 'Fear not, for **I have redeemed you**; I have called you by your name; You are Mine.'"*

~Heart Caption~

Recently I came across a hymn titled "I'm Redeemed" written by T. C. O'Kane in 1884. Read the words along with me. I pray the second verse captures your heart as it did mine:

I'm Redeemed – T. C. O'Kane
O, sing of Jesus, "Lamb of God," Who died on Calvary.
And for a ransom shed His blood, for you and even me.

I'm redeemed, I'm redeemed, through the blood of the Lamb that was slain, I'm redeemed.
O, wondrous power of love divine! So pure, so full, so free!
It reaches out to all mankind, embraces even me.

I'm redeemed, I'm redeemed, through the blood of the Lamb that was slain, I'm redeemed.

All glory now to Christ the Lord, and evermore shall be;
He hath redeemed a world from sin, and ransomed even me.

I'm redeemed, I'm redeemed, through the blood of the Lamb that was slain, I'm redeemed.

The phrase "I have redeemed" means to pay a price for something or someone, to pay a price that could not be paid by the thing or person who is or was held captive. When I think of and meditate on the words redeemed and ransom, the picture comes to mind of the price that was paid for the salvation of humanity. As the saying goes, if there could be an actual price that was placed on salvation, the rich would live and the poor would die. During the Passover and Easter season, I love to go back through the Scriptures and read about the Passion of our Savior, demonstrating His love for you, me, and humanity, recalling to my mind the actual price that we were ransomed for. One Scripture that leads me into this reading is Hebrews 12:2 which says, *"Looking unto Jesus, the author and finisher of our faith, who for the joy that was set before Him endured the cross, despising the shame, and has sat down at the right hand of the throne of God."*

While meditating on Christ's sayings during His suffering, the following phrase was continuously whispered in my heart: ***See, I have redeemed you.***

From the moment of the preparations for Passover, the breaking of bread, the serving of the wine, the moments of the First Communion, even throughout the moment of exposure of His betrayer, Christ's words continued to whisper in my heart: ***See, I have redeemed you.***

Through the walk to the Garden of Gethsemane, through every moment of agony of spirit that His sweat fell to the ground like great drops of blood, through the times of prayer where the disciples' flesh was weak but their spirit was certainly willing, I continued to hear Christ's words whisper in my heart: ***See, I have redeemed you.***

With a kiss, He was handed over to those who would crucify Him and He willingly went, even healing the soldier's ear which Peter cut off. Yet I still could hear Christ's words whisper in my heart: *See, I have redeemed you.*

Even as He was dragged from courthouse to courthouse, beaten, punched, spat upon, questioned, tried like a criminal; yet I continued to hear Christ's words whisper in my heart: *See, I have redeemed you.*

With Peter's denial fresh in His mind and heavy upon His heart, He moved through the crowds as the solders pushed Christ down the Via De La Rosa. I still hear Him say: *See, I have redeemed you.*

With every slap of a hand to His face, every punch of someone's fist to His body, and even when He was scourged, I hear Him lovingly say: *See, I have redeemed you.*

As He watched as the solders tie his wrists and nail them to each beam of the cross, I hear His gentle whispers: *See, I have redeemed you.*

Through the crushing pain of the nails as they pierce the first wrist, then the second wrist, in agony my Lord screams out in pain. Even today, the scream ripples throughout time and I still hear Him say: *See, I have redeemed you.*

As the soldier's eyes moved down past Christ's arms, torso, and upper thighs following the trail of blood, there is a moment of silence as the earth attempted to take in the brevity of experiencing and hearing its Creator struggle in pain. As the Creator is crucified, His heart looks to the joy of you and me that was set before Him according to Hebrews 12:2. He whispers: *See, I have redeemed you.*

~Focus Point~

See, 1 have redeemed you

Here is your chance; here is a place where victory is written out in the pages of your life and history! Write out what Christ has redeemed you from. By your God-given authority and by the blood of Jesus, denounce everything that once held you captive and acknowledge dominion over it.

In the name of Jesus, I have been REDEEMED and I have authority and dominion over…

_____

_____

_____

_____

By the blood of Jesus Christ and the word of my testimony, I overcome in the following areas, moment by moment, day by day because Satan no longer has authority or dominion over my life. The strings and attachments of these entrapments are broken, burned at the root by the fire of God. In Jesus' name, I soar and am triumphant over every last challenge.

Write the areas that you are believing God for the manifestation of victory in your life:

_____

_____

_____

_____

Layer One ~ Day Seven

Daddy, Keep Silent

Isaiah 43:1
"But now, thus says the LORD, who created you, O Jacob, And He who formed you, O Israel: 'Fear not, for I have redeemed you; ***I have called you by your name; You are Mine.'"***

~Heart Caption~

In my family, almost every child is given a nickname. My oldest son was called Foodie, and my daughter was called Sugar, though my youngest son was able to escape having a nickname. To this day, my sister is still lovingly called Stay. I was often called NaeNae by my family.

Beloved, you, too, may have acquired some names during your past. Some of those names may have followed you into your present. Consider this truth: our Heavenly Father calls us by our name. His name for us is different than our given name. What a privilege that the God of the whole earth calls you ***Son*** or ***Daughter***! The God of all creation also calls you ***Friend***. John 15:14 says, *"You are My friends if you do whatever I command you."* The God who created time calls you ***Chosen***. First Peter 2:9 says, *"But you are a chosen generation, a royal priesthood, a holy nation, His own special people, that you may proclaim the praises of Him who called you out of darkness into His marvelous light."*

God does not compare you to anyone else. He sees you as YOU. He knows the names of all the stars and galaxies and the names of the snowflakes. He knows the names of the angels, and beloved, He knows you! He knows you intimately and loves you so much that He calls you ***Beloved***.

~Focus Point~

Isaiah 43:1
*"But now, thus says the LORD, who created you, O Jacob, And He who formed you, O Israel: 'Fear not, for I have redeemed you; **I have called you by your name; You are Mine.**'"*

It may be that family, friends, and those who never meant the best for you have also called or labelled you by a name. They may have also called you out of your name. They may have called you names with the intention to decree and declare over you curses and evil forebodings. But God's word over you is higher, and His word over you is eternal. Anything less has fallen to the ground and has been burned up by the fire of God in Jesus' name. Therefore, look and take note of some names God has called you to counteract and abolish evil names others may have called you.

People called you ugly, but God says….
"You shall also be a crown of glory In the hand of the LORD, And a royal diadem In the hand of your God."
Isaiah 62:3

People called you unloved and unlovable, but God says….
"Behold what manner of love the Father has bestowed on us, that we should be called children of God! Therefore the world does not know us, because it did not know Him."
1 John 3:1

People called you left, abandoned, and a reject, but God says...

"But you are a chosen generation, a royal priesthood, a holy nation,
His own special people, that you may proclaim the praises of Him
who called you out of darkness into His marvelous light."
1 Peter 2:9

People called you a name because they really didn't know YOU.

"For Jacob My servant's sake, And Israel My elect,
I have even called you by your name; I have named you,
though you have not known Me."
Isaiah 45:4

Write down additional names your heavenly Father calls you:

_____

_____

_____

_____

God makes a declaration over our lives – our faults, our upsets, our
discounts, our wavering, our mistakes, and our challenges – and
says to us, "No matter what, you are Mine and I love you." We do
not belong to ourselves. We do not look to ourselves. We do not
depend upon ourselves. Our hope and our trust is not in ourselves; it
is in our heavenly Father who created us, loves us, cares for us, and
watches over us. Even when we do not think He is looking, He sees
and He hears us. Psalm 34:15 says, "The eyes of the Lord are on the
righteous, And His ears are open to their cry." He knows where we
have come from and where we are going. We belong to Him.

Layer Two ~ Father to the Fatherless

Layer Two ~ Introduction

Father to the Fatherless

Words like **Father, Daddy, Dad, Poppa, Pop,** or even **Abba** are words that do not readily roll off my tongue. I have to be intentional about saying these words, and I am intentional about saying them to God. Although I have had a father, when I was less than three months old, my father's life was snatched away from him. Unfortunately, there never arose a man to take his place. Therefore, I have never seen, had, nor imagined a "father-figure" in my life. I have a spiritual father, and I thank God for him. To have a human father in your life who continuously has your heart, and you have his heart, is something genuinely special. Honestly, I didn't know what a father or daddy was supposed to look like. Yet in my heart and soul, I yearned for something. I didn't know what it was that I was yearning for until I was well into my late forties and God began to awaken a longing that I had submerged under years and layers of hurt, rejection, fear, abuse, misuse, shame, guilt, and even pride.

God began to awaken feelings of missing something, missing someone that I had never experienced. I didn't know how to feel or even categorize the feelings. I was only able to recognize the longing of my heart after years of prayer, worship to God, and the peeling back of layer after layer of dysfunction so that I really could heal, and I could no longer hide behind the smile and the pretense that everything was okay. Nothing was fine, and nothing was working out alright. I was hurting, but I needed help to identify the source of my pain. Even then, once the source of my pain was identified, how do I go about bringing relief to the pain that consumed me and was the biggest part of how I acted, reacted, and went about doing life? I had to learn.

This is the journey that God took me on. I'd be lying if I said that it was a fun journey; it was not. There were times that I didn't know whether I was coming or going. There were times that I was so numb that if someone asked me what hurt, I couldn't accurately identify the pain because I hurt all over. But God – my Abba, my heavenly Father, brought healing and deliverance. To be honest, He is still bringing healing and deliverance to my life, even now as I write. But I would be lying if I said that it was not a process. In fact, it has been more than just a process. Join me in the journey. I pray that as you continue to participate in this devotional, you, too, will be made whole, moment by moment, day by day, and layer by layer.

Layer Two ~ Day One

Father to the Fatherless

Psalm 68:5
"*A **Father of the fatherless**, a defender of widows, Is God in His holy habitation.*"

~Heart Caption~

The complaint of most, if not all, parents with their first child is that they had no "manual" on how to raise their new baby – what to do and how to do it, how long to feed, when to let the baby nap, how long he/she should sleep, etc. How do I tell when something is wrong, or how do I know when things are right? Although my father was not in my life, my heart was grafted into the Kingdom of God and the Lord became my Heavenly Father. I would often say to God, "But Father, I don't know how to be a daughter. I've never been taught 'how' to be a daughter." Where do I go to look up how to be a daughter? In my cries to God, He would say to me through His Word, "I am your Father and I will guide you with my eye."

Psalm 32:8 says, "*I will instruct you and teach you in the way you should go; I will guide you with My eye.*" The word for "teach" means to instruct, direct, teach, point, shoot, aim, throw, or cast in a straight manner. God is our Father. One of the Hebrew words for father, *ahv*, also means father or producer of a certain thing, which is related to the Aramaic word *abba*. Many believers refer to God as Abba Father. This not only means producer of a thing, but also originator and creator. The Lord God is our heavenly Abba Father, and He is the creator, our originator, and our producer of the life and breath that is within our body. He instructs, directs, teaches, points us in the right way, aims us in the direction we should go, and casts us in a straight manner to move forward.

But when you're trying to be something or work something up according to what you have seen or heard, that's not you. You're looking at someone else and trying to adapt who you really are so that you will be accepted and loved. I had to learn that my heavenly Father loves me. He created me. I am the work of His hands. I am his workmanship, as it says in Ephesians 2:10, *"For we are His workmanship, created in Christ Jesus for good works, which God prepared beforehand that we should walk in them."*

Our heavenly Father is our Creator. He desires to write the story of our lives as an artist writes a poem or draws a picture. God desires that we surrender our lives to His workmanship. He knows the plans that He thinks towards us (Jeremiah 29:11). He desires to write and draw out for you and me a plan and a purpose. It is not too late for God to make a masterpiece out of your life! God desires to reveal His plans and purposes, especially those which He desires to put into motion with our acceptance of Him as Savior, Lord, and Father. Once He has been granted access to the seat of the throne in our heart and all other former occupants of the throne of our heart are removed, He can begin to direct our lives.

~Focus Point~

In envisioning the focus point for today's devotional, a picture of a chair, perhaps a lounge chair that we have in our bedrooms, was impressed on my heart. As this chair is in our bedroom, we may tend to have clothing items on this lounge chair; perhaps a shirt, pants, or other clothing items that we have worn during the week. We place them on the chair because we have worn them and thus will need to have them cleaned. Perhaps we even have some books or reading materials on the arm of this chair. This chair is so cluttered with other items that we are no longer able to sit in the chair ourselves. Often, just as that chair in a very personal space such as our bedroom is cluttered with clothing items, books, etc., so our heart may have become cluttered as well over the years. We may find ourselves on the seats of our own hearts – our ideas, our desires, our dreams, and our ambitions. There are other things on the seats of our heart such as attitudes, actions, relationships, finances, difficulties, tragedies, and troubles. All of this is sitting on the throne of our hearts and is directing our lives in one way or another. God says to us, "Allow My love to purge these things from your heart, and allow Me to come in and do life with you." God desires that we would allow Him to strip the chair of our heart clean from those things that take precedence in our hearts and in our lives. God desires preeminence! God desires to sit on the throne of our hearts, comforting, consoling, and counseling us, not second but first.

If you have not already done so, invite Jesus Christ into your life. Invite God the Father to sit on the throne of your heart.

Revelation 3:20
"Behold, I stand at the door and knock. If anyone hears My voice and opens the door, I will come in to him and dine with him, and he with Me."

If this is your first time receiving Christ as Savior, write out your personal prayer asking Jesus to come into your heart.

_____

_____

_____

_____

On this day, I have received Jesus into my heart: _____

If you have previously accepted Christ as your Savior, do you find your heart, like the chair or other piece of furniture in your private bedroom, is cluttered with your own ambitions, attitudes, hurts, maybe disappointments? Write out a prayer, asking Christ to clear the clutter and take preeminence in your heart and life once again.

_____

_____

_____

_____

Layer Two ~ Day Two

Father to the Fatherless

Psalm 68:5
*"A Father of the fatherless, **a defender of widows**, is God in His holy habitation."*

~Heart Caption~

In Luke 7:11-15, we read the story of the widow of Nain and her son:

> *Now it happened, the day after, that He went into a city called Nain; and many of His disciples went with Him, and a large crowd. And when He came near the gate of the city, behold, a dead man was being carried out, the only son of his mother; and she was a widow. And a large crowd from the city was with her. When the Lord saw her, He had compassion on her and said to her, "Do not weep." Then He came and touched the open coffin, and those who carried him stood still. And He said, "Young man, I say to you, arise." So he who was dead sat up and began to speak. And He presented him to his mother."*

Jesus was arriving back from Capernaum when he came near to the village of Nain. Nain was a small town off the main road and was approximately 20 miles from Capernaum. Upon approaching the city gate, Jesus was met by a funeral procession of people carrying the body of a young man followed by his weeping mother. The woman had already lost her husband, and I imagine that the loss of her only son was utterly devastating. She was now alone. During this time in history, as a part of the Jewish community, men and women married in their early teenage years and bore as many children as they could as this secured the family's inheritance. As the parents grew older, they depended upon the children, specifically the sons, to work the farm or the family business and carry the family name throughout generations. Women were not allowed to own property, so if a woman lost her husband and sons, she was reduced to beg for her sustenance and be at the mercy of the place where she lived. The community might help the widow, though in a small town such as Nain, things were hopeless for her.

Yet, Jesus departed from the main road and was intentional about arriving into the town just as the burial processional was arriving at the city gate. What a divine interception! Just as the widow was leaving the city to bury her only son and all hope for her was leaving the city on that death bed, Christ walks into the city **_with_** all hope, stops the death procession, and goes directly to her and says to her, *"Do not weep."* Christ then goes to the death bed, touches the dead body, and says to the widow's son: *"Young man, I say to you, arise."* The custom of that day was that if anyone touched a dead body, they were considered unclean. However, Jesus is not governed by the ritual cleansing of Him touching the dead body. He was more concerned with the compassion that He felt and the pain that He saw and knew for this widow. He immediately identified with the pain and loss she was experiencing.

Later in Scripture, as He was dying on the cross of Calvary, John 19:26-27 tells us, *"When Jesus therefore saw His mother, and the disciple whom He loved standing by, He said to His mother, 'Woman behold your son!' Then He said to the disciple, 'Behold your mother!' And from that hour, that disciple took her to his own home."* Jesus knew and understood the fate of widows of His day. He did not leave that heart-wrenching fate for His own mother, nor did He leave that same fate to the widow of Nain.

Often when we think of people who Jesus raised from the dead, our hearts immediately go to Jesus' friend Lazarus. But the son of the widow of Nain did not know Jesus. The widow did not know Jesus, and yet He was even more intentional about getting to the widow and her son, before they left the city's gate, to bring him back to life. The widow was not left to leave the city with no hope. Jesus, full of compassion for her, met her at the place of hopelessness and filled her with all hope by raising her son back to life!

Jesus defended the widow of Nain from the spirit of hopelessness. When all hope was quickly evaporating from her life, Jesus intentionally met her and surrounded her with all hope!

~Focus Point~

Beloved, are you alone? Are you without a husband, without a son, a daughter, or even a friend? Has your life left you feeling alone or hopeless? Our heavenly Father is a Father to the fatherless; Jesus is a friend to the friendless **_and_** a defender of widows. Are you experiencing challenges in your life where you desire Christ to come in and bring relief to the areas where you may feel alone, hopeless, frustrated or challenged in your life?

Write out a prayer telling your heavenly Father what you are experiencing; leave nothing out. Share your heart with the Father, full and free, and invite Him in to bring all that He is to your situation and circumstances.

_____

_____

_____

_____

Ways I recognize that my Heavenly Father is stepping in to help me:

_____

_____

_____

_____

Layer Two ~ Day Three

Father to the Fatherless

Isaiah 64:8

*"But now, O LORD, **You are our Father**; We are the clay, and You our potter; And all we are the work of Your hand."*

~Heart Caption~

Have you ever had a conversation with God where you were talking with Him and He was responding back immediately? Perhaps it felt like you were talking with your closest friend. He was just as near to you as your very skin. The moment was intimate and yet charged. Your heart was burning with every word that He was speaking. You felt that time had passed; surely, it has been more than an hour, even two, that you have been in this posture of the heart with God. After moments of silence, you lift your head, your eyes come back into focus, and you realize that it's been just a few minutes. Remain still in the presence of the Lord and allow Him to do His inner work on your mind, your heart, your eyes, your ears, and your mouth. The Lord is our Father, and He desires to look at us, look upon us, and examine every fiber of our being. This happens as we are in His presence, remaining still, reading His word, listening, and receiving His divine impartation.

We are the clay in the hands of our great God, our potter. We are the work of His hands. Allow the potter to complete the work that He has begun in your life. Remain still on the potter's wheel in your silent, quiet time, and allow the great potter to complete His work.

~Focus Point~

During your time of prayer with the Lord, choose to linger in His presence. Remain there in His presence. Dwell in His beauty. As the presence of the Lord begins to console and comfort you, write down words and phrases that the Holy Spirit speaks to you, and meditate on them.

_____

_____

_____

_____

_____

_____

_____

_____

Layer Two ~ Day Four

Father to the Fatherless

2 Corinthians 6:18
"I will be a Father to you, And you shall be My sons and daughters, Says the LORD Almighty."

~Heart Caption~

Today's verse is so beautifully and innocently written and appears to be of no harm. In fact, it is encouraging until you read the context preceding it. 2 Corinthians 6:11-18 reads:

> O Corinthians! We have spoken openly to you, our heart is wide open. You are not restricted by us, but you are restricted by your own affections. Now in return for the same (I speak as to children), you also be open. Do not be unequally yoked together with unbelievers. For what fellowship has righteousness with lawlessness? And what communion has light with darkness? And what accord has Christ with Belial? Or what part has a believer with an unbeliever? And what agreement has the temple of God with idols? For you are the temple of the living God. As God has said: "I will dwell in them And walk among them. I will be their God, And they shall be My people." Therefore "Come out from among them And be separate, says the Lord. Do not touch what is unclean, And I will receive you."
>
> "I will be a Father to you, And you shall be My sons and daughters, says the LORD Almighty.'"

You cannot be a part of Kingdom living and act like paupers in the land. There is a difference in a king's kid and a pauper's kid. By definition, a pauper is a destitute person except by charity. A pauper is a person who grew up with nothing and has the mindset of nothing. Inwardly, they have received themselves as poor and not having anything. They do not have a general or adequate supply of clothes nor a decent place to live. They often have to scrape and scrap for their very existence. They do not live a privileged life. As my mom would say, "They do not have a pot to piss in nor a window to throw it out of." On the other hand, the king's kid has that and more. A true king's kid first and foremost has an assurance of who their father is; they know that royalty runs through their veins. They recognize their importance in the world simply because their father has assured them of such importance, not their name but the presence of their father! They are privileged because of the love that their father has for them. This love spills over into every area of their lives. They are always assured of the Father's love for them; it's in their heart.

Because we are children of the Almighty God, we walk, act and live as children of God, not to perform for His love but because of His love for us.

~Focus Point~

I am a king's kid. Because I am a child of the King with a great inheritance, I decree and declare that:

My heart is and will forever be open to the Lord Jesus Christ!
I make an active decision to not team up with those who are unbelievers.
I make an active decision to not partner with wickedness.
I no longer choose to live with nor walk or live in darkness, but I will walk as the light of righteousness for my generation.
I no longer choose to be a believer who partners with an unbeliever.

I choose to be in sync and in union with God because I am the temple of the living God.

Based upon the following paraphrase of 2 Corinthians 6:16-18, write out your own confession and declaration below.

God will live in me.
God will walk in me.
God will be my God.
I will be a part of the family of God.
Therefore, I will come out from among unbelievers, and separate myself from them.
I will not touch their filthy things, and the Lord will welcome me.

_____

_____

_____

_____

Layer Two ~ Day Five

Father to the Fatherless

Psalm 103:13 (NLT)
"The LORD is like a father to his children, tender and compassionate to those who fear him."

~Heart Caption~

The Lord is *like* a father. The word "like" is defined by Dictionary.com as: of the same form, appearance, kind, and character. So we could read this as the Lord is of the same form, appearance, kind, or character to a father. Who better to know the intimate compassions, security, and strength of a father than the Heavenly Father who created the first father Adam? The Heavenly Father knew the intricacies of the role and personhood of a father. The Heavenly Father is the master father and maker of all fathers. Our earthly father has faults, may have at some point in his life rebelled against the perfect will of God, and may have refused to own up to his rights, authorities, and role as a father. But our Heavenly Father steps in and becomes ***like a father*** to us as His child, tender and compassionate to us in love and sincere kindness. The love of God permeates our very being and transforms us from a daughter or son without a father to a child of God. We are children of our Heavenly Father.

~Focus Point~

The word *like* is permeating my heart. My heart is intrigued by the word *like*. What is the character of our Heavenly Father? Meditate on Psalm 103:13 (NLT), write it down, and pray it. *The Lord is **like** a father to his children...*

_____

_____

_____

_____

_____

_____

_____

Layer Two ~ Day Six

Father to the Fatherless

John 1:12-13

"But as many as received Him, to them He gave the right to become children of God, to those who believe in His name: who were born, not of blood, nor of the will of the flesh, nor of the will of man, but of God."

~Heart Caption~

Have you received Christ? In receiving Him, He has given you the "right" to become a child of God! You have a legal right; you have been adopted into the royal family of God. The Scripture above says: *"...to those who believe in His name..."* Do you believe in the name of the Lord Jesus Christ for your salvation? If you believe <u>and</u> accept Jesus as your savior, you have rights. You have legal rights in the Kingdom of God, apart from the kingdom of darkness.

Just as those in the United States have a legal right to the benefits as residents of the U.S. as well as those in different cities, states and townships. A U.S. citizen has rights that others who are not U.S. citizens cannot claim nor take part in. There is such a thing as an illegal alien in the United States. An illegal alien is defined by Dictionary.com as "a foreigner who has entered or resides in a country unlawfully or without the country's authorization." With this definition in mind, here is even a more pointed definition as noted by Dictionary.com regarding an illegal alien: "a foreigner who enters the U.S. without an entry or immigrant visa, especially a person who crosses the border by avoiding inspection or who overstays the period of time allowed as a visitor, tourist or businessperson." To bring this point further into focus, in John 10:9, Jesus begins His dialogue about being the True Shepherd: *"I am the door. If anyone enters by Me, he will be saved, and will go in and out and find pasture."*

As we enter the Kingdom of God by the name of Jesus Christ, we will be saved, and we will go in and out and find pasture. We must be born again just as Jesus spoke to Nicodemus in John 3:7, *"Do not marvel that I said to you, 'You must be born again.'"* We can't make this happen by our own wills nor by our own might or strength, God's Spirit invisibly does its work inside our hearts. We can't see it happening, but we can see the results of this beautiful work. Once we are born again, we have legal rights in the Kingdom of God. We are adopted into the family of God, and the rights and inheritance for a child of God are made available to us as believers. The promises of God have become promises that we can claim. The assurances of God begin to manifest in our lives. Our relationship with God through the Lord Jesus Christ is actively manifested through the Holy Spirit and is lived out in our daily lives through prayer, reading of the Scriptures, and our lifestyles.

~Focus Point~

We are children of God! Everything that our loving Father has destined for us through the fellowship of Jesus Christ is made available to us. We receive tangible blessings of God as part of the family of God. Some of those spiritual blessings include:

- Peace which surpasses all understanding (Philippians 4:7)
- Being blessed with every spiritual blessing in the heavenly places in Christ (Ephesians 1:3)
- Being chosen by Him before the foundation of the world, being holy and without blame before Him in love (Ephesians 1:4)

- Being predestined to the adoption as sons by Jesus Christ to Himself, and accepted in the Beloved (Ephesians 1:5-6)

I am captivated by God's love and longing for us as children of God. God loved us from the foundation of the world. We are legally a part of the family of God, and we are heirs and joint heirs of our heavenly Father's Kingdom. We are not illegal aliens, but we are citizens of the Kingdom of God, for Ephesians 2:19 says, "Now, therefore, you are no longer strangers and foreigners, but fellow citizens with the saints and members of the household of God."

When we believe and receive the Son, Jesus Christ, we are sealed until the day of Jesus Christ with the Seal of Holy Spirit (Ephesians 4:30).

Layer Two ~ Day Seven

Father to the Fatherless

Psalm 27:10
"When my father and my mother forsake me, Then the LORD will take care of me."

~Heart Caption~

To those who may feel void of care and love because they have been abandoned and/or rejected by your mother, your father, or perhaps both parents, I know how that feels. My father was killed by his wife when he confessed to her that I had been born after having an affair with my mother. Although I was an infant at the time and I have lived my entire life without my earthly father, I have learned that God fills the gaps of our lives, especially in the place as a mother and/or a father. He does not leave us as orphans to figure out life on our own. Throughout His Word, God gives us verses of Scripture for those who have experienced such a loss. For example:

- "I will not leave you orphans; I will come to you." (John 14:18)
- "The LORD watches over the strangers; He relieves the fatherless and widow; But the way of the wicked He turns upside down." (Psalm 146:9)
- "He administers justice for the fatherless and the widow, and loves the stranger, giving him food and clothing." (Deuteronomy 10:18)

I have witnessed friends tell stories of the Lord's deliverance, help, and strength in times of need as they depended upon Him as a heavenly Father. They tell of His direction and His guidance during times of sovereign appointment, providing spiritual motherly and/or fatherly care, especially for those who may have experienced life in the foster care system. Nothing is impossible for God. He is our heavenly Father, and He works on our behalf to take care of us, His children.

~Focus Point~

Record times in your own life when you may have experienced a void, abandonment, and/or rejection, and you watched God step in and provide for you as the loving Father that He is:

_____

_____

_____

_____

Write out a prayer of thankfulness for God rising up and showing Himself strong on your behalf in the situation and/or challenge you noted above.

_____

_____

_____

_____

Layer Three ~ Delayed Growth

Layer Three ~ Introduction

Delayed Growth

A father's presence and his role in the life of a child are critically important. A loving and involved father supports the mother and the child and provides emotional, psychological, educational, and developmental growth to be experienced and affirmation received by the child. Unfortunately, when this role is absent from the home, the effects grow and expand throughout the child's life, especially if the role of the father in some form is not made available to the child. For me, the absence of the love of my father was crucial, even critical, in my life.

Layer Three ~ Day One

Delayed Growth

1 Peter 2:2
*"As newborn babes, **desire the pure milk of the word**, that you may grow thereby."*

~Heart Caption~

The word "thirsty" is a saying in today's culture. Although the base of the meaning of the word thirsty from Dictionary.com is "feeling or having a thirst to drink" or the **need** to drink, in some sub cultures, the word also means *someone* longing, desiring, craving, or being *over eager* to have something or someone. In this sense, the picture comes to mind of a person chasing after another person, a person chasing after a particular job or position, or someone longing for a platform and willing to do anything to get it. Other more positive forms of "thirsty" is one who is hungry for their destiny, thirsty for the anointing of the Holy Spirit, and thirsty for God's presence.

In the letter of 1 Peter, a longing church in the middle of severe persecution is told to render themselves as a newborn baby whose only desire is to drink, long for, and thirst for the pure *milk* of the Word of God. The Apostle Peter never tells them to long for promotion. The Apostle Peter never tells them to fight for, chase after, desire, or be "thirsty" for other people, status, platforms, positions, or postures whereby they themselves are exalted. The posture of the heart that the Apostle Peter yearns for us to take is in his first three words: as newborn babes. We are to desire, yearn for, long for, crave, and be thirsty for the pure and undefiled milk of the Word of God. Do not even desire meat; that will come as you continue to grow in your faith and naturally mature as a believer. First and foremost, you need to have the milk of the Word of God which provides adequate and appropriate calcium for teeth, enabling you to grow strong for chewing meat, and to grow strong bones for standing solidly. But you first and foremost must desire the milk of the Word of God **so that you may grow by the Word of God.**

~Focus Point~

With sincere honesty, examine your place in life right where you are, here and now. What were you thirsting for that led you to this place?

_____

_____

_____

_____

As you are now thirsting for the Word of God and you are growing in the knowledge of your Lord and Savior Jesus Christ, what are some desires, aspirations, and ambitions you are believing the Lord will allow you to accomplish?

_____

_____

_____

_____

Layer Three ~ Day Two

Delayed Growth

2 Peter 1:5-8
*"But also for this very reason, **giving all diligence, add to your faith virtue, to virtue knowledge**, to knowledge self-control, to self-control perseverance, to perseverance godliness, to godliness brotherly kindness, and to brotherly kindness love. For if these things are yours and abound, you will be neither barren nor unfruitful in the knowledge of our Lord Jesus Christ."*

~Heart Caption~

Since we have now obtained this precious faith in our Lord and Savior Jesus Christ, now let us add to our faith. The Apostle Peter says now that you have come into the grace of a saving experience in Christ, there is more. We have not ___arrived___ since coming into our salvation. In fact, there is much work to be done. In 2 Peter 1:5-8, we are provided steps to take to pursue Christ, grow in our relationship with Him, and become a faithful witness to and in the Body of Christ.

The first step that we are given is "giving all diligence." The word diligence is a noun and it can mean haste, earnestness, or careful and persistent work or effort. Synonyms for the word diligence are conscientious, industrious, and rigor. The Apostle Peter says to be diligent to add to our faith; work hard and be conscientious about adding to our faith. Friend, there is a work that must be done; however, if we are lazy, this won't happen. If we're looking for quick results, this won't happen. We have to be careful, persistent, and diligent.

In our working and being diligent, now let us add to our faith virtue. The word virtue here is found used in classic Greek writings and it means moral goodness, excellence, and purity. The Apostle Peter, in his gentleness of Spirit, encouraged believers to be careful to work hard and not be lazy with our faith. Do your part by adding moral goodness, excellence, and purity to your life, which will be exemplified in your walk as a Christian.

It's beautiful that the Apostle Peter doesn't stop there. That's not all that there is; he adds on phrase after phrase. Do your part by working hard and being diligent to add moral goodness, excellence, and purity of life. Add to this knowledge of God (a seeking to know, inquire, and investigate general intelligence and understanding), just as it says in 2 Peter 1:2: *"Grace and peace be multiplied to you **in the knowledge of God,** and of Jesus our Lord."* Seek to know God, inquire in the Word of God, and through prayer, give your heart to knowing God, His ways, His attributes, His characteristics, and His heart.

~Focus Point~

Before any kingdom work is done outwardly, there must first be an inward work within the person pursuing Christ and His Kingdom. The process of such work is laid out for us by the Apostle Peter as quoted above – being diligent to add to our faith moral goodness, excellence, and purity of life along with a seeking to know God in and through His word. These are spiritual blessings, according to Ephesians 1:3: "Blessed be the God and Father of our Lord Jesus Christ, who has blessed us with every spiritual blessing in the heavenly places in Christ." However, we must access them by adding them to our faith.

Make a list of characteristics and virtues regarding moral attributes, excellence, and purity of life and meditate on how you can add them to your faith.

_____

_____

_____

_____

Research Scripture references regarding the characteristics and virtues noted above and pray them over your life.

_____

_____

_____

_____

Layer Three ~ Day Three

Delayed Growth

2 Peter 1:5-8
*"But also for this very reason, giving all diligence, add to your faith virtue, to virtue knowledge, **to knowledge self-control, to self-control perseverance**, to perseverance godliness, to godliness brotherly kindness, and to brotherly kindness love. For if these things are yours and abound, you will be neither barren nor unfruitful in the knowledge of our Lord Jesus Christ."*

~Heart Caption~

In life, we have endured scars, scrapes, and scabs due to events such as learning to crawl, walk, falling down, and getting back up. As we continue to grow, we find ourselves with bumps and bruises from situations and circumstances that have happened to us throughout our journey in life. We have endured much in our lives, and all the challenges that we have experienced have hopefully taught us lessons such as not to touch a hot stove, not to play with scissors or knives, and not to date your best friend's man or woman. Life's lessons are to teach us not to draw back but to help us learn from the mishaps and move forward.

However, if we're not careful, drawing back is just what we tend to do. We draw back so that we do not experience the pain again. We draw back because we do not want to experience the rejection again. One simple lesson that is hard to learn is that without risk, true living does not exist. We tend to forget that if you're still breathing after the hurt, you can go on in life and become better. Unfortunately, sometimes, we stop short of beginning again.

As the believers of the early church faced difficult or even perilous times, they, too, were moving from a life as an unbeliever, becoming believers by the grace of God, and learning the heart of God. They had come through life's experiences and traumas. They had the bruises and scars to prove it. Some were dealing with emotional challenges, just as we are in this current day and time. Peter speaks to them about growing as God would desire them to grow. He encouraged them to not simply grow outwardly, but mainly to grow inwardly and spiritually. Thus he says that in view of all that God has given you, all that pertains to life and godliness, by which we have been given exceedingly great and precious promises, we have a role in this as well. We are participators in what God is doing in and through our lives. We are to add, complement, enhance, improve, and increase our faith with virtue – moral, ethical, wholesome, decent, and honest character, goodness, and excellence of superior quality. We are encouraged to add to our faith moral, ethical, decent, proper, and honest behavior of superior quality.

The Apostle Peter does not stop here but he presses us on to add to our faith self-control (the ability to control ourselves, our mouths, and our minds), and then to persevere in doing so. The word "persevere" assures me that this active participation of adding self-control does not mean that it's a one-time deal. This is ongoing. We think that once we have "tied our bow tie," that we're safe; all is good and the water is running from the well sufficiently. But this is not so. There is still work to be done, and that work continues in our lives until we take our final rest in the Lord.

We do this work by reading the Word of God and other books that encourage spiritual growth and discipline. We do this work by drawing near to God through prayer, fasting, and necessary spiritual disciplines. We do this work by practicing the presence of God and walking in the Spirit. This work is our ability to continue to grow and develop into the person of character that God has appointed for us.

During the many seasons of our lives, we are encouraged to continue to grow and develop – academically, emotionally, spiritually, not just physically.

We are not to simply say that we accept Christ as our Savior and sit idly by and not develop our faith. We are to add to our faith and thereby grow into the beautiful Christian, the child of God that He has called us to be.

~Focus Point~

Are there instances in your life where a trauma happened, and you have not fully recovered from the pain or the hurt which you were exposed to? If so, describe the situation and how it affected you.

_____

_____

_____

_____

_____

_____

Did this situation cause you to give up and never try again? Did this circumstance stunt a level of growth in your life? If so, what was stunted? What level of growth was arrested?

_____

_____

_____

_____

Now that you know God has given to you all things that pertain to life and godliness, He desires for you to get up and move forward. By His strength, one moment at a time, one day at a time, take steps toward adding to your faith. Recognizing this, what are the steps that you personally will take to add to your faith?

_____

_____

_____

_____

Layer Three ~ Day Four

Delayed Growth

2 Peter 1:5-8
*"But also for this very reason, giving all diligence, add to your faith virtue, to virtue knowledge, to knowledge self-control, to self-control perseverance, **to perseverance godliness, to godliness brotherly kindness, and to brotherly kindness love**. For if these things are yours and abound, you will be neither barren nor unfruitful in the knowledge of our Lord Jesus Christ."*

~Heart Caption~

When you hear the word godliness, what comes to mind? For some they might immediately begin to think of hair coverings, long dresses, ankle-length skirts, no make-up, quiet and non-combative demeanor, no movies, no bowling alleys, no earrings, etc. These are what I used to think of when I thought of "godliness." However, these are simply outward displays that have nothing to do with one's heart's posture. Christ is more concerned with our heart's posture than our outward adornment. In fact, these were some of the problems with the priests of His day known as the Pharisees and Sadducees; Christ identified them as white-washed tombs (Matthew 23:27). These people looked godly; they had the outward look of self-righteousness, but inwardly their hearts were corrupt.

In light of this, when Peter tells the church to add "godliness" to our faith, what is he talking about? One thing is for sure, he is not speaking of running to take the hem out of your dress so that it hangs as low as your knees or touches the floor. There is no need to do this if your heart is not changed and it is filled with lust, greed, pride, and everything else that would lead you down a road to ungodly behavior and then hiding it. Here is the problem: If a man convinces you to raise your skirt or dress past your thighs, what good has looking godly benefitted you? If you look the part of a holy man and you carry yourself around others as a holy man of God, yet you beat and mentally abuse your wife, what good has looking godly benefitted you?

The characteristics that the Apostle Peter is instructing us to add are characteristics that have little to do with our outward looks. The African American community has dwelt long and hard on "looking" the part. Even in the late 1970s and early 1980s, we were preached to that we should "fake it until we make it." This is all a part of the look good society that was supposedly saying to our neighbors, "See how good I'm doing? I'm failing inwardly but outwardly, I look really good." This is not, nor will it ever be, God's heart for His people.

To be sure that we're adding exactly what God is instructing us in His Word, let's look at the definition of godliness. One interpretation is written as, "indicating reverence manifested in actions", according to the Blue Letter Bible and Vines Expository Dictionary of New Testament Words. This means that your reverence for God, the Word of God, and the people of God is *demonstrated in your actions*. Godliness becomes a part of you and is to be walked out in your daily life. It must be *demonstrated in your actions* as you walk it out both in the private areas of your life and outwardly as well, so that you are not an outward success and a private failure. This is godliness; the truest sense of integrity is who you are when no one is looking.

This helps and gives you the *supernatural ability* to walk in brotherly kindness – kindness to others whether you know them or not. Hebrews 13:2 says, *"Do not forget to entertain strangers for by so doing some have unwittingly entertained angels."* It's almost like the Scriptures are giving you steps; do not leap to love but take steps. The first step is adding to your faith godliness, having reverence for God, His Word, and His people, which is demonstrated in your actions. This will lead to brotherly kindness. The demonstration of your actions moves you closer to brotherly kindness, followed by the next step of love. This is not easy; human beings are sometimes difficult or challenging to love. It's not easy, but it's not impossible.

God makes this measure of love, this measure of godliness, possible through walking by the Holy Spirit. We can't do this in our own strength nor by white knuckling it. It will take the strength and the power of the Holy Spirit to accomplish this. The Word of God tells us in Galatians 5:16, *"I say then: 'Walk in the Spirit, and you shall not fulfill the lust of the flesh.'"* If we rely upon the Holy Spirit to enable us, pray, and yield to His supernatural ability to move us forward in this endeavor, we really can do it.

~Focus Point~

Sometimes, people have been so used to being hurt, rejected, disappointed, and angry that they inflict pain on others because of their own pain. They do not walk in love or even demonstrate outward acts of kindness to others, let alone themselves. Write down some ways that you can be nice, be kind, and demonstrate acts of kindness toward yourself.

_____

_____

_____

_____

Write down some ways that you can be nice, be kind, and demonstrate acts of kindness toward others.

_____

_____

_____

_____

Do you need to contact someone that you have been especially unkind to? Out of the newfound love of Christ in your heart, do you need to demonstrate an act of kindness toward them? If so, begin by writing about it here.

_____

_____

_____

_____

Layer Three ~ Day Five

Delayed Growth

2 Peter 1:5-8

"But also for this very reason, giving all diligence, add to your faith virtue, to virtue knowledge, to knowledge self-control, to self-control perseverance, to perseverance godliness, to godliness brotherly kindness, and to brotherly kindness love. ***For if these things are yours and abound,*** *you will be neither barren nor unfruitful in the knowledge of our Lord Jesus Christ."*

~Heart Caption~

The Apostle Peter is instructing us to add to our faith a generous provision of moral excellence, knowledge, self-control, patient endurance, godliness, brotherly affection, and love for everyone. **"For if <u>these things</u> are <u>yours</u> (ours) and abound..."** These faith characteristics must be yours – not your pastor's, not your pastor's wife, not your mentor, not your coach, not your best friend, not your husband, not your boyfriend, not the lady who does your hair, not the postal man who delivers your mail, not anyone else's, but **YOURS**. It's written this way because this is a relationship. It is a very personal relationship between you and your Lord and Savior, Jesus Christ. We are only responsible for ourselves, our own actions, and our own beliefs, not those of anyone else.

~Focus Point~

A lot of what we do and/or need to do is built on the foundation of taking ownership of our growth and relationship in Christ. How are you moving forward in achieving "these things"?

_____

_____

_____

_____

If these faith characteristics are yours and abound – **thrive, flourish, overflow, and are plentiful** – you will <u>not</u> find yourself lacking, needy, thirsty, wanting, nor missing out. You will flourish and grow in your relationship with Christ, your Lord and Savior.

I no longer want to live my life from a place of comparison to other Christians because I am needy, thirsty, and/or wanting something that I think they have and feel that I'm missing out on, instead of growing in my own relationship with Jesus Christ. My desire is to be plentiful in my love for God and for His people.

What steps can you take to add to your faith to ensure your personal relationship with Christ is flourishing and you are growing and being fruitful?

_____

_____

_____

_____

Layer Three ~ Day Six

Delayed Growth

2 Peter 1:5-8
*"But also for this very reason, giving all diligence, add to your faith virtue, to virtue knowledge, to knowledge self-control, to self-control perseverance, to perseverance godliness, to godliness brotherly kindness, and to brotherly kindness love. For if these things are yours and abound, **you will be neither barren nor unfruitful** in the knowledge of our Lord Jesus Christ."*

~Heart Caption~

I have read and reread the above Scripture, and when I got to the words "you will be neither barren nor unfruitful," something deep within my soul stood still. I know what it is to give birth to three beautiful babies. I understand what it is to give birth to a ministry calling and watch it flourish as though the wind of God was at its back, pushing and propelling it forward. I know what it is to be productive at work and watch my job and my name on the job become fruitful because of God's faithfulness in my life. I know what it feels like to go from living at the lowest of life's lows and move from there to being fruitful both in my income and in my family. I continue to experience God's goodness and Him causing me to be fruitful against all odds in my life. I know what it feels like to be productive and come from the bottom and see a little "rise" in my life; praise God, to Him be all of the Glory!

However, going through a pandemic in 2020, remaining in isolation for months, and continuing well into 2021 with seemingly no end in sight causes you to really look deep within yourself and have some truthful and real conversations that you were "too busy" to have before the pandemic. I've been having such conversations with the Holy Spirit, especially as I began writing the companion book to this devotional. These conversations caused me to revisit some very hard places in my life, especially as I began to recall situations and circumstances that brought about deep hurt, resentment, pain, bitterness, and unforgiveness.

What does this have to do with being barren and unfruitful? As we are growing in our personal relationship with Jesus Christ, learning and speaking with the Holy Spirit, and allowing Him to shed light on areas that we are to delve into, we add to our faith virtue, and to moral goodness knowledge and self-control. I began to consider where I am both emotionally and spiritually. I had to be truthful with myself and the Holy Spirit and say it: I've become barren. Entering the pandemic season of 2020, I had to admit that although my life appeared to be full and productive, I was barren.

I have experienced being fruitful in several aspects of my life, and yet when the pandemic began in March 2020 and life as we knew it came to a screeching halt for some of us. There were many of us who had to stop our physical and mental busyness. We filled our lives up with meetings, places to go, people to see, and other things that prevented us from having a heart-to-heart talk with God. However, when there is no place to go and no one wants to see you for fear of spreading a virus to them, you may find yourself like I did – a home that's almost completely empty and a cell phone that does not ring with calls nor text messages. I felt that I was no longer on people's radar. I'm no longer too busy for my own britches. Now the Holy Spirit was saying to me, "I've got you just where I want you; can I have a moment of your time?" The Holy Spirit began revealing to me through the Scriptures that yes, I had grown, but the Father was pruning me even more so that I could be even more fruitful. I can't begin to tell you how easy it is, if you're not careful, to become complacent, lazy even and settled in your "Christianity." You may think to yourself that you have just finished a devotional, so you're on your way, life is sweet, and your fruit is ripe for the picking. You have checked all the boxes. My hunger had become satisfied with devotions containing Scriptures in the Old Testament, the New Testament, one chapter of the Psalms, and one chapter of Proverbs. I had become satisfied with my morning prayer; it was sincere, but not effectual, not fervent, and not on fire. It didn't leave me wanting more; it was mediocre, like an obligation, not like my life depended on it.

However, after a couple of weeks in the pandemic, the Holy Spirit was continuing to impress upon my heart Revelation 3:15: *"I know your works, that you are neither cold nor hot. I could wish you were cold or hot."* He impressed upon me that He desired me to come out of the pandemic better than how I entered it. He impressed upon my heart a continuous seeker's perspective, to seek Him continuously and fervently, to search for Him in the Scriptures and not have a Bible app do all the work for me, to cry out for Him with my own voice. We as human beings tend to become lax and lazy when our work becomes someone else's work.

I took back the reins and began crying out on my own. I began adding to my faith virtue, knowledge, self-control, perseverance, godliness, and brotherly love. I stopped waiting on my phone to ring or a text message to come through. I began praying for the saints and reaching out to those the Lord impressed upon my heart, checking in on them to see if I could serve them. I began hungering and thirsting for righteousness. Christ, through His Word, began to fill me with the Holy Spirit once again with a new fire and a new passion. Sometimes I said words in my prayers, but more times than not, I was simply groaning and moaning because I didn't know what or how to pray for all the challenges that I and others were facing. Romans 8:26 says, *"Likewise the Spirit also helps in our weakness. For we do not know what we should pray for as we ought, but the Spirit Himself makes intercession for us with groanings which cannot be uttered."* This pursuit of the Holy Spirit and His perfect will for my life brought me to a place of being fruitful and no longer barren in Him. I'm still on my journey of growing in Him, and this is a holy fire that I am continuously praying will never go out.

~Focus Point~

My cry to the Holy Spirit is to set me on fire. He will ignite your flame, but you must tend to the fire. You must keep your fire burning bright.

Are you on fire for Christ? Why or why not?

_____

_____

_____

_____

If you need to rekindle your fire for Christ, what are actions that you need to take to do so?

_____

_____

_____

_____

Remember that it is not your pastor's, nor your prayer leader's, nor anyone else's responsibility to keep your flame burning brightly. The quickest way to lose our focus is by giving someone else the responsibility that lies at our door.

Layer Three ~ Day Seven

Delayed Growth

2 Peter 1:5-8

*"But also for this very reason, giving all diligence, add to your faith virtue, to virtue knowledge, to knowledge self-control, to self-control perseverance, to perseverance godliness, to godliness brotherly kindness, and to brotherly kindness love. For if these things are yours and abound, you will be neither barren nor unfruitful **in the knowledge of our Lord Jesus Christ."***

~Heart Caption~

As you grow and develop in Christ, your life becomes productive, meaningful, and preserved by the sustaining power of God. One of the ways that this happens is in and through the Word of God abiding in your life – the knowledge of our Lord and Savior Jesus Christ being made alive and quickened within your spirit. This causes you to grow, develop, live, walk, and talk in this world but to not be of this world. We live and breathe the air of planet earth, however it is the daily breath of God which breathes life into our spirit. It's the daily walk in the Word of God that washes over us, cleanses us from all sin, and keeps us pure and holy, living and walking upright before Him. It is the joy of the Lord that gives us strength; daily keeping us moving and thriving and igniting the flame of the Holy Spirit in our hearts. As we continue to fervently seek Him and His way of doing life, we grow in the knowledge of our Lord Jesus Christ.

~Focus Point~

In Jesus' priestly prayer before His crucifixion, He prayed for the apostles and those who would be won to Christ by their words and prayers, including us as New Testament believers. Read the below verses and rewrite them **inserting your name** (instead of "them" and "they"). Make John 17:14-19 a daily prayer:

I have given them Your word; and the world has hated them because they are not of the world, just as I am not of the world. I do not pray that You should take them out of the world, but that You should keep them from the evil one. They are not of the world, just as I am not of the world. Sanctify them by Your truth. Your word is truth. As You sent Me into the world, I also have sent them into the world. And for their sakes I sanctify Myself, that they also may be sanctified by the truth.

_____

_____

_____

_____

_____

_____

_____

_____

_____

_____

_____

_____

_____

Layer Four ~ Unhealthy Exposure

Layer Four ~ Introduction

Unhealthy Exposure

Unhealthy exposures are plans derived from the enemy of your soul and sent to destroy you; however, they have been thwarted by God! Unhealthy exposures may have touched your life, but they do not have to stop you from living. The unhealthy exposures of our lives can thrust us toward the Holy Spirit and cause us to render ourselves totally submitted to Him for divine exposure. Divine exposure is when the Holy Spirit comes into your life, reveals His promises and purposes for your life, and lets you know that your story does not have to end where you thought it was over.

Layer Four ~ Day One

Unhealthy Exposure

Psalm 54:1
"Save me, O God, by Your name, And vindicate me by Your strength."

~Heart Caption~

Save me, O God! God, help me! HELP! Maybe one of these cries for help was what you yelled, screamed, moaned, or perhaps silently whispered to yourself as you were being exposed to pornography, to the sexual parts of a friend or even a relative.

Unhealthy exposure can look different ways to different individuals. For me, it looked like being exposed to unhealthy and unfamiliar touching by a family member who taught me how to read, write, and count. It was unhealthy whispering, touching, and breathing while I was writing the alphabet on 3-rule lined paper. This was being done by a familiar and trusted person who was exposing me to fear, shame, regret, hurt, disappointment, and unwelcomed sexual advances. This started for me as a child and continued well into my tween years. The lifestyles that I developed, disappointing life choices that I made, fear, shame, regret, hurt, disappointment, and low self-esteem were all manifestations of these unwelcomed sexual advances and molestation. This created an environment of loss-acceptance whereby I accepted everything that happened to me, whether good, bad, or indifferent. This was what I knew and understood at that time, and for me, that was my identity.

But when I was crying out for help, God was there. When you were crying out for help, God was there, too! I find that we don't often admit this because we can't explain that if He really was there, why did He allow such tragedy? We don't have all of the answers as to why we had to go through those difficulties and traumas. One thing I have learned in my healing process is that although the Lord did not cause it, He will use it to bring glory to His name. Romans 8:28 says, *"And we know that all things work together for good to those who love God, to those who are the called according to His purpose."* The working together is a process, and we all have to go through our process. Rest assured that the promise of God stands true: although He did not cause it, He will use it to work together for the good of those who love God, for those who are the called ones according to His purpose.

David, the sweet psalmist of ancient Israel, cried out in Psalm 54:1, *"Save me oh God by Your name, and vindicate me by Your strength."* Perhaps you may have thought, "Lord, no one knows, recognizes, nor respects my name. In fact, it's because of the shame of my name, the shame and the dishonor and the curse that was on my family name deep within my bloodline, that this is happening to me." But you cry out to your Lord, "God, save me by Your name! Vindicate me." David cried out this word vindicate, which means to justify, support, uphold, or defend. You may not even have known to cry out this prayer. Maybe your prayer was simply, "God, HELP!" I didn't know enough to even make this plea. But now, being on the other side of things, being much older and understanding more, we cry from our hearts and make our petitions known before the Lord. Unhealthy exposures of our childhood may have happened years ago, but the consequences which resulted and manifested may be ongoing emotionally, spiritually, physiologically, and psychologically.

When the psalmist David fought the giant Goliath early in his life, he had three smooth stones in his arsenal of weaponry. By the power of Almighty God, only one smooth stone was needed to take out Goliath long enough for David to chop off his head. The smooth stone in our arsenal known as "By Your Strength, Lord" will knock out our Goliath long enough for us to chop off its head as well. Goliath was bigger and stronger than David, but Goliath was no match for

David's God! Nor is our goliath a match for our GOD! We do not fight our Goliaths by our strength; our strength is in the name of the Lord. By the strength of our God, we will take down every Goliath, every mountain, and every circumstance that comes up against us – not by our might nor our strength, but by the strength of the Lord. By Your strength, Lord God!

~Focus Point~

Are you currently faced with the unhealthy exposures of your life still robbing you of a healthy future? Cry out to God about them here:

_____

_____

_____

_____

What has God spoken to you about going forward? What does moving forward look like to you?

_____

_____

_____

_____

Did you feel an unexplainable peace and release in talking to God and getting His perspective, direction, and guidance regarding this situation? Write your thoughts.

_____

_____

_____

Layer Four ~ Day Two

Unhealthy Exposure

Psalm 54:2
"Hear my prayer, O God; Give ear to the words of my mouth."

~Heart Caption~

God, do you hear me? God, are you listening to me? These are questions that we may not feel comfortable asking in a room filled with other believers. In fact, we may only ask these questions when we're alone or with our closest of friends. Does God hear me? Is what I'm saying and what I'm even going through worth Him listening to? Some of us may discount our worth and value because of the situation that we find ourselves in and what we've done or have been through in life. Perhaps you believe that no one has heard the loud inner screams of your heart, let alone God. You may even believe that no one hears you, let alone sees you, and definitely not God.

Beautiful one, I say to you that people may have placed their hands over your mouth to cover up your screams, but God heard your cry from every fiber of your being. No one can silence your heart's cry to God, the maker of heaven and earth. Remember the story in Genesis 4:9-10, where God talks to Cain about him killing his own brother, Abel: *"Then the LORD said to Cain, 'Where is Abel your brother?' He said, 'I do not know. Am I my brother's keeper?' And He said, 'What have you done? The voice of your brother's blood cries out to Me from the ground.'"*

I say to you, lift up your head, beautiful one; God can hear your voice. If he heard Abel's blood crying out from the ground, surely he can hear your muffled cries. God can hear the words that you are not saying – the words you hold back, the disappointment, the fear, the mistake that you shy away from. God hears you. Stop thinking and believing that you are not heard or that you are not even seen. Psalm 139:7-10 says: *"Where can I go from Your Spirit? Or where can I flee from Your presence? If I ascend into heaven, You are there; If I make my bed in hell, behold, You are there. If I take the wings of the morning, And dwell in the uttermost parts of the sea, Even there Your hand shall lead me And Your right hand shall hold me."*

From the heights of every mountain to the depths of life, despair, and all points in between, God has proven Himself, and He remains faithful. He is there. He hears you, beautiful one. My question to you is, are you crying out to Him or are you crying out to man, to woman, or to the "system"? Neither man, woman, nor the "system" can answer you in the intricacies of life; but in everything, if you seek God, He will hear and answer you.

~Focus Point~

Are you looking for God to come through for you, or have you placed your trust in another human being?

_____

_____

If you have placed your trust in someone else to hear you, listen to you, and come through for you, repent. Tell God that you're sorry and return to Him for He will hear your faintest cry. He really will answer you, but you have to turn to Him.

_____

_____

_____

_____

Layer Four ~ Day Three

Unhealthy Exposure

Psalm 54:3

"For strangers have risen up against me, And oppressors have sought after my life; They have not set God before them. Selah"

~Heart Caption~

Have you ever had problems with your own family members? Have you ever had problems with folks who pretended to love you (or at least like you), and when their hearts were revealed, they actually hated you more than their own enemies? This was the problem David was experiencing in Psalm 54. David was having hate problems with members of his own tribe, the Ziphites. Instead of sticking up for David, they were selling him out and giving him away to his enemies! In Psalm 54:3, we find David at the heart of the matter. Instead of David saying to God, my family has risen up against me, He said, *"For strangers have risen up against me, and oppressors have sought after my life."* Those strangers and oppressors David was talking about were people of his own tribe and could very well have included his cousins, his uncles, his aunts, his nephews, and his nieces. This hurt David to his core, so much so that he called the people who rose up against him, members of his own tribe, ***strangers*** and ***oppressors***. They turned on him in such a way that he didn't even recognize them.

That's what sin does. Sin gets down in the heart of people who should love you, or at least support you, but the sin in their heart turns them against you. It's a hard pill to swallow when your own family rises up against you. It's a deep root of hurt when your own family, let alone your friends who you thought were with you, stands up, comes out of hiding, and cuts you down like a tall tree.

This is the unimaginable pain that some of us have faced. Our own family members may have exposed us to unhealthy situations and circumstances. Perhaps they do not even seem like family to us because they appear as strangers and oppressors due to the hurt, shame, and the turmoil that they have caused in our lives. This is what David meant when he said that they have risen up against him. He didn't expect them to do what they were doing. This insult, this hurt, came out of nowhere.

Can you relate? The situation that you may find yourself in, the arrow that has struck you in your heart, may have come from a family member, and it may have almost drained the life blood out of you. But this is very true and needs repeating: the enemy of your soul will use whoever is available to extinguish your fire! The enemy does not know God's plans for your life. The enemy cannot tell the future! But because you are made in the image of God, the enemy hates you. Every time the enemy sees you and hears you, you remind him that you were created in the image of God. You are in the earth with a body, spirit, and soul and are given the choice to both acknowledge and serve God with all of your heart. Friend, that right there is fire to the enemy, and he wants to put out your fire. But your fire cannot be extinguished. **Your fire was given to you by the Holy Spirit, and He increases your flame.** Glory to God! Your enemy targeted you for destruction from the moment your earthly father fertilized the seed of your mother in her womb. He will use anyone, absolutely anyone within his grasp, to make that happen, whether friend, family, or foe.

Beloved, when you are a child of God, you belong to Him. Let that sink in before you move on to the next sentence. **You belong to God. You are not alone**. We are not alone, nor do we have to fend for ourselves. We are children of Almighty God, and He takes care of us. David talked to the Lord because He could. David prayed, sat quietly, and meditated on the Lord's faithfulness to him because he could! No matter where David found himself, nor what he was going through, he knew that he belonged to God and God had the final say. Your enemy does not have the final say, friend. God is in control, and He speaks over our lives.

~Focus Point~

In the hurt and pain that you have endured, you may feel abandoned and alone. Imagine God Himself *reading to you* a bedtime story from Psalm 54:1-3. Hear Him say to you:

Verse 1: "Save me, O God, by Your name, and vindicate me by Your strength."
God says: *I am here to save you Daughter, Son, by My name, and I will vindicate you by My strength.*

Verse 2: "Hear my prayer, O God; Give ear to the words of my mouth."
God says: *I hear your cry. I heard you when you first began to cry out to Me. I hear the words that are coming from your heart, not only from your mouth.*

Verse 3: "For strangers have risen up against me, And oppressors have sought after my life; They have not set God before them. Selah"

God says: *I know those who were closest to you may have hurt you, and it seemed they desired to destroy your life. Remember, you belong to Me and I will take care of you. I will defend you.*

Layer Four ~ Day Four

Unhealthy Exposure

Psalm 54:4
"Behold, God is my helper; The Lord is with those who uphold my life."

~Heart Caption~

After all that David had encountered up to this point in Psalm 54, at this point it's as though he quiets himself, calms down, and says to himself, *"Behold, God is my helper."* David uses the name for God "Elohim," which is the same word used in Genesis 1:1. This refers to God as the great creator, the beginner, the author, and our Father! He is here and HE is my helper! David says that his spirit is alive with the fact that he has seen and experienced extremely painful things in verses 1-3 of Psalm 54, but right here in this present space, he realizes that God, Elohim, is his helper. Elohim is all that I need. I do not need an army; I just need to calm myself down and see that Elohim is my helper!

Not only does David encourage himself with this phrase but he goes on to say, *"The Lord is with those who uphold my life."* The Lord, the one to whom I have submitted my entire life, soul, and spirit, is with those who uphold my life. My Lord is with those who support, uphold, sustain, refresh, and revive me. Remember, by this time in his life, David had amassed a small army of Mighty Men who were faithful to him to the death. David says that his Lord is **with them** that uphold, support, sustain, refresh, and revive my soul. These guys were

81

the real and true "ride or die," or in other words, best friends forever. David could not repay them for their sacrifice. More than likely, there was no monetary or tangible reward for their love demonstrated to David, and he realized this. But David gave them something better. He confessed over their lives, "*My Lord is with them that uphold me.*" This is at its truest form a rich and satisfying blessing because David does not only pray and encourage himself, but after he is built up, he turns and blesses those who have held him up. This is what true love does, and this is exactly what David did.

Beloved, you have not made it this far without those friends, even if just a few. Look back over your life, thank God, and bless those who may even be nameless or faceless but they gave a kind word, put a few dollars in your hand, or may have even provided some advice that you didn't adhere to at that time. Thank God for them! These people arc thc ones who were used by God to get you from one point to the next, and now, turn and pray for them. Ask God to bless, cover, shield, provide for, support, strengthen, and keep them.

~Focus Point~

Father, you remember those who have stood with me, even against those who told them not to support me. I offer up this prayer for them and their families. Father, allow our paths to cross in the future so that I can personally have a face-to-face encounter with them to let them know that I appreciate their efforts and am praying for them.

_____

_____

_____

_____

Begin to list them by name if you know them personally. If not, simply and sincerely begin to pray for them.

_____

_____

_____

_____

It may initially be hard to do, but I encourage you to pray prayers of release and forgiveness for those who you may know or believe may have said or spoke words of discouragement towards you and your family.

_____

_____

_____

_____

Layer Four ~ Day Five

Unhealthy Exposure

Psalm 54:5
"He will repay my enemies for their evil. Cut them off in Your truth."

~Heart Caption~

As a young girl, I remember seeing fights where a kid lost, but by the time he or she got home, their siblings told their mom what had happened, and the mother would take him or her back outside and tell him or her to fight the other kid: fight him or her until he or she won the fight. Perhaps you may have been raised in a culture as I was, where we were taught by our parents that if someone were to hit you, you were to hit them back. If you didn't think that you could beat them, pick up something, anything, and bust them upside their head. This brings tears to my eyes even as I think and write about it now. Ultimately, we were taught to seek retribution for ourselves. We were instructed, even spitefully permitted, to seek retribution on our own behalf or on someone else's behalf if we felt obliged to. This is a trap that the enemy has laid out for us.

In Psalm 54:5, David gives us an invitation to look further in 1 Samuel 26 where he is being chased, hounded, and sought after, for no reason at all, other than King Saul's jealousy, which ultimately was being fueled by the king's fear of David. Yet, David was determined to not render evil for evil and reward King Saul with the same bitter vengeance that he was dishing out.

Now, in your present circumstances, do you feel that you are being chased, hounded, or hunted down by the situations and circumstances in your life? Do you act on your own accord, or do you allow God to repay your enemies? Although we may have had help getting into our circumstances, perhaps we wish we would have just as much help getting out of them. Who is the person who wronged you? Perhaps you may not even have known it until further down the road that they did you wrong. It hurts when this happens. But what do you do with the pain that you now feel? The _what_ of what they did and the _who_ it was that did it are both painful!

Friend, God sees your pain. He saw the incident even before it happened, and He sees the end of the matter as well. You may even be going or growing through it right now, even as you read this devotional. It may seem as though the fat lady has sung her last song, and everything is over and done with, but not according to God. Beloved, God has the final say. Galatians 6:7 tells us that we reap what we sow: *"Do not be deceived, God is not mocked: for whatever a man sows, that he will also reap."* Or as the saying goes, "What goes around, comes around."

I have learned this lesson on several fronts. Sometimes it was easier to learn than at other times, but when you let God repay what has been done, He repays it well, better than we ever could. Remember, God is our vindicator! When God repays, you do not have to add your two cents to the matter, and you also do not have to look over your shoulder and watch to make sure only your shadow is following you. We used to fight with sticks and stones, but when God fights, He fights with His truth! John 17:17 says, *"Sanctify them by Your truth. Your word is truth."* His Word is the truth. Second Corinthians 10:4 says, *"For the weapons of our warfare are not carnal but mighty in God for pulling down strongholds."*

We do not need to fight. We need to turn the situation, the circumstance, and the people involved over to God. He will tell you through His Word to forgive, release, and let them go. Release them and the situation from your emotional prison. In doing this, you release and let yourself go, and you are free of them. You no longer torment yourself by holding them hostage in the prison of your mind and your heart. God will repay them however He sees fit. You do not have to instruct God on how to deal with folks or how to repay them. Talk to God and pray them right out of your mind and into His heart.

~Focus Point~

Read these passages from a heart that is ready to see forgiveness with fresh eyes and an open heart:

Luke 17:3 says, *"Take heed to yourselves. If your brother sins against you, rebuke him; and if he repents, forgive him."*

Matthew 6:14-15 says, *"For if you forgive men their trespasses, your heavenly Father will also forgive you. But if you do not forgive men their trespasses, neither will your Father forgive your trespasses."*

Matthew 18:21-22 says, *"Then Peter came to Him and said, 'Lord, how often shall my brother sin against me, and I forgive him? Up to seven times?' Jesus said to him, 'I do not say to you, up to seven times, but up to seventy times seven.'"*

This is my prayer for you, friend: Father, You are our Friend, Counselor, and Comforter, and you remain closer to us than our own relatives. We can be honest with You in saying that a person has hurt us or that this situation has taken the wind out of us. Father, You know all things. We do not know their motives, but acting solely upon your Word, Lord, we choose to forgive them. We choose to forgive them and the situation, not only so that we can receive forgiveness from You for our sins but also so that we can let them go. We release them to You so that You can fill our hearts with love and peace for them.

But Father, if our heart is filled with hate and unforgiveness for them, there is no room for Your love and Your peace. Father, we need Your love. We need Your peace.

Father, pour out Your love upon them so that instead of the enemy imprisoning them, they would feel Your love. Father, Your Word declares that it is the goodness of God that leads men to repentance. Father, I pray Your goodness upon them. Lord God, surround them that they, too, may see Your goodness, repent, and turn from their ways to You. Father, I pray that the light of Your love would shine all the more in our hearts for them and others like them. When the enemy reminds us of this situation, Father, help us to recall Your Word of forgiveness and this heartfelt prayer that we continue to pray for them that we both may be free in Jesus' name. Amen!

Write out your own prayer and experience God's healing power as you do:

_____

_____

_____

_____

Layer Four ~ Day Six

Unhealthy Exposure

Psalm 54:6
"I will freely sacrifice to You; I will praise Your name, O LORD, for it is good."

~Heart Caption~

Have you ever experienced someone's overwhelming goodness towards you or your family? I'm not trying to over spiritualize this, but have you ever experienced someone's genuine overwhelming goodness towards you and the only thing you could think of was how you could repay them? Perhaps you thought of asking, "What do you need?" "What do you want?" or "What can I give, get, pick up, or purchase for you?" Perhaps you ask what you can do for that person simply because you're so very grateful for what they did.

This was David's response in Psalm 54:6, "I will freely sacrifice to You; I will praise Your name, O LORD, for it is good." I will sacrifice to you of my own free will. You do not have to ask for it; Your goodness has overwhelmed me so that I want to give you all of me, Lord. Your goodness and Your kindness have simply overwhelmed me that I want to bless, celebrate, and call out Your name as loud as I can – truly, You are good!

When you are faced with a situation that only God can bring you out of and no one else can deliver you but God, He shows up and ends up doing exceedingly and abundantly more than you ever expected. You didn't know how to ask for what God did on His own accord. That's just how good He is and has been to us all. Simply because of His immense goodness, we offer our lives as a free will offering to live holy, acceptable, and pleasing lives as a living sacrifice before Him. Think about it; nothing that we could ever give God can be more precious to Him than our lives! We can't offer God money; He owns the cattle on all of the hills. No amount of money can compare to a holy, acceptable, and pure life that only you could offer before the Lord God.

Give Him your life, beloved! This is the only and best sacrifice that you could ever present to Him – sacrificially, willfully, and pleasingly.

~Focus Point~

Romans 12:1
"I beseech you therefore, brethren, by the mercies of God, that you present your bodies a living sacrifice, holy, acceptable to God, which is your reasonable service."

What have you tried to give to God, only for Him to say, "I just want you"?

_____

_____

_____

_____

What does presenting your body as a living sacrifice look like to you?

_____

_____

_____

Layer Four ~ Day Seven

Unhealthy Exposure

Psalm 54:7
"For He has delivered me out of all trouble; And my eye has seen its desire upon my enemies."

~Heart Caption~

The confident conclusion

As I read and reread David's declaration in Psalm 54:7, I hear faith speaking. Each time I read it, I hear faith speaking louder and more confidently! *"For He has delivered me out of all my trouble…"* David was speaking through the eyes of the Holy Spirit. Psalm 54:7 is not the end of David's writings, nor is it the end of his troubles. Because David had faith in the God whom he served, he proclaimed just as he had done many times before that He has delivered me. David had many more battles to fight, many more betrayals, and many more losses, yet he confidently said, *"For He has delivered me out of all trouble."*

I encourage you to read the book of Psalms chapter by chapter and study it, meditating slowly on each verse. In your study, read through commentaries that can provide the backstories which inspired each psalm. You will discover that often David, who wrote many of the psalms, began the psalm in deep despair, however by the end of the psalm, a change had taken place and David chose to speak by faith; he chose to proclaim the triumphant end.

Isn't that what God does on our behalf? He has declared our end from our beginning. We may have had a rough start for the first 20, 30, 40, or even 50 years of our lives, and yet God steps in and says to us through Isaiah 46:10, *"Declaring the end from the beginning, And from ancient times things that are not yet done, Saying, 'My counsel shall stand, and I will do all My pleasure.'"* David knew that he was a servant of God and that he was anointed by God. Because of his assurance of who God had proven Himself to be in his life, David had confidence that God would do what He said He would do. God promised to deliver him out of all of his troubles. In Psalm 27:3, David declares, *"Though an army may encamp against me, My heart shall not fear; Though war may rise against me, in this I will be confident."* David had been at this place several times, and truth be told so have we. Perhaps you have been here before where you didn't see your way clearly, where you didn't see how things were going to work out. But through the Holy Spirit, you stayed in the presence of God. In His Word and by faith, He once again allowed you to see the end of your challenge(s).

Beloved, you, too, will see as David did at the very end of Psalm 54:7: *"For He has delivered me out of all trouble; and my eye has seen its desire upon my enemies."* However, do not let this be your focus. David knew what it was like to defeat his enemies – lions, tigers, bears, and even Goliath! But remember, in the New Testament, we fight differently! Recall to mind 2 Corinthians 10:3: *"For though we walk in the flesh, we do not war according to the flesh."* We do not fight as David did, in the flesh. We fight in the Spirit. We fight with the Word of God through prayer in faith and perseverance.

~Focus Point~

Life may have had a challenging start for you, and this exercise may be challenging for you to do, but this is where faith steps in. List your challenges and then list God's deliverance from each of them. Go as far back in your life as you can. After you have listed the challenges and the deliverance, write out a personal thank you to God.

Layer Five ~ Self-Esteem

Layer Five ~ Introduction

Self-Esteem

Who are you really? Do you know who you are, really? You have been squeezing who you are into the mold that the culture, society, your present friends, your job, and/or your social media friends have dictated that you should be. Believe me, you cannot change who you really are to be friends or to get along with and be accepted by someone who really does not know or like who you are at your core. Who you really are is God's gift to everyone around you, if you would be authentically YOU.

Layer Five ~ Day One

Self-Esteem

Ephesians 2:10
"For we are His workmanship, created in Christ Jesus for good works, which God prepared beforehand that we should walk in them."

~Heart Caption~

When God created you and me, He created us as a masterpiece, a work of art! Our Heavenly Father created us in Christ Jesus to do good works. These good works can be described as beautifully prearranged acts which are ordered by God to help and assist others in ways that bring Him glory. Philippians 1:6 says, *"being confident of this very thing, that He who has begun a good work in you will complete it until the day of Jesus Christ."* The word good in both Ephesians 2:10 and Philippians 1:6 is the Greek word *agathos*, and it means good in a physical and a moral sense and producing benefits. The word *agathos* also has a synonym *kalos*, which means good in an aesthetic sense, suggesting attractiveness and excellence. Both of these verses not only complement one another but also confirm their meaning about God's creation, His masterpiece. As His work of art, our decree could read like this:

> I decree and declare that I am God's masterpiece, His work of art, created in Christ Jesus to do good, beautiful, prearranged acts, established from the foundation of the world. These beautiful acts are physically attractive and morally excellent works, all for His glory.

Ephesians 2:10 could be paraphrased as: My Heavenly Father equips me. His grace enables me, and His Holy Spirit fortifies, strengthens, and builds me up in Christ Jesus in order to do so.

I give glory to God for the beautiful work He has called me to do.

Layer Five ~ Day Two

Self-Esteem

Psalm 139:14

"I will praise You, for I am fearfully and wonderfully made;
Marvelous are Your works, And that my soul knows very well."

~Heart Caption~

How beautiful you and I are to our Heavenly Father! When He looks at us, He does not question Himself, nor does He doubt what He has made nor His decision about creating us. We began as a thought in the mind and heart of God, where all life springs forth. He created our inward parts and knit us together in our mother's womb, according to Psalm 139:13. We are a work of art; Ephesians 2:10 says that we are God's masterpiece, His poem. He displays us for His glory. With every birth and cry from the womb, God's praise is, "Look at my creation!" You, His beautiful creation, are fearfully and wonderfully made!

There may be discomforting stories surrounding your birth and the birthing process that your mother and father may have had to go through in order for you to be born, but nothing could stop you from making your entrance into the earth realm. It was necessary that you be here at such a time as this. The enemy may be trying to convince you that your birth was unimportant. Friend, your birth was and is important. God chose you to be born in the current time that you are living in. God could have had you to be born in the 1600s, in the 1800s, or in another part of the world, but God chose you to be born in this time and in the location that you were born in. God also handpicked your parents. Friend, you were no accident.

God did not look at you and say to His Son and the angels, "Let us go back to the drawing board, we have made a mistake." No; when God created you, He smiled. He knit all of your intricate parts together beautifully, according to the Scriptures. You are fearfully and wonderfully made by your Creator, Jehovah God. Nothing was overlooked when He created you.

Instead of complaining or not fully appreciating your outward and inner beauty, let us change the negative narrative of ourselves from this day forward. Let us only speak of how beautiful we are. Let us agree with the Word of God as it proclaims His truth over our lives:

~Focus Point~

Thank you for making me so wonderfully complex!
Your workmanship is marvelous – how well I know it.

Write out some "focus points" of your outward and inner beauty and give thanks to God for them.

_____

_____

_____

_____

Layer Five ~ Day Three

Self-Esteem

Song of Solomon 4:7
"You are all fair, my love, And there is no spot in you."

~Heart Caption~

Do you know anyone who would say to you, "Everything about you is beautiful; you are without a flaw"? No one but a mother or father, right? When a parent looks at their newborn child, still wrapped within their arms and covered by love, what do they see? Nothing but love. When a husband looks at his wife and a wife looks at her husband, they see his or her beauty. Even the flaws that may be visible to others are covered by the love that the husband or wife have for their mate.

Our Heavenly Father says this to you and me, "You are all fair, my love, and there is no spot in you." Where people have picked out our visible flaws and characterized them by making us aware of them and attempting to make us feel bad about them, our Heavenly Father, through His word and by His Spirit, continues to remind us that, "You are all fair, my love, and there is no spot in you."

How is it that we have come so far in life that we believe a person's word over what our Heavenly Father says about us? If we believe people in this aspect, what else are we believing from people instead of our Heavenly Father?

~Focus Point~

Everything that our Heavenly Father created is good – everything. Our Father created male and female in His image. Genesis 2:7 says, *"And the LORD God formed man from the dust of the ground, and breathed into his nostrils the breath of life; and man became a living being."* We were made in the image of God and carry His breath within our very being. There is no flaw in our creator God. We may not be perfect, look perfect, or feel perfect, but we are loved beyond measure by the God who made the universe. What someone else sees from their standpoint concerning you may not be pleasing or favorable to them; nevertheless, in the eyes of our heavenly Father, we are without flaw.

Friend, I have eyes like my heavenly Father – eyes that see the beauty in creation and humanity. I do not see as man nor woman sees; I choose to see as my heavenly Father sees, through the eyes of love. What about you? How are you choosing to see things?

I am made in the image and likeness of my heavenly Father, and He calls me beautiful. He calls you lovely. He loves me and you, and His presence rests upon us, His creation, in great measure.

Name some of your imperfections and declare the beauty of the Lord over each and every one of them.

For me: I have Ujamaa nappy hair, yet in the center of my illustrious locks is a bald spot that I have covered up for years, although each year it becomes more difficult to do so. Nevertheless, my declaration is: my hair is thick, beautiful and a glorious crown upon my head.

Now you: Write out what you see as your imperfections and declare God's beauty in and through each one:

_____

_____

_____

_____

Layer Five ~ Day Four

Self-Esteem

Psalm 139:16
"Your eyes saw my substance, being yet unformed. And in Your book they all were written, The days fashioned for me, When as yet there were none of them."

~Heart Caption~

God saw you and me before we were born. In my imagination, He looked upon us, smiled gently, and nodded His head while we were still yet an embryo – not as yet born. He looked upon us with love and a Father's heart. He did not have to see the full figure of our face to see us as beautiful. Nor did He have to see all of our ligaments, count our toes, see our eyes blinking, or see us smile. We were just an embryo and He loved us. He loved us so much that His love made us want to grow, no matter how long it took; we wanted to grow and see the hands that created us and fashioned us, formed us in our mother's womb. We wanted to see our Heavenly Father. Our Heavenly Father's heart planned and scheduled our days and our nights before we took one breathe. He recorded His desires in His book.

Do you know that God has books that He keeps in heaven? The book of Revelation speaks of a book with names in it and a book with works in it (Revelation 20:12). God has books where He has made and kept a record of every day and of His desires for you and me. Remember Jeremiah 29:11: *"For I know the thoughts that I think toward you, says the LORD, thoughts of peace and not of evil, to give you a future and a hope.* " God's books are filled with His plans.

We may have gone astray from God's desires that were recorded in His book, but God did not throw us away. No, He watched over our lives, drawing us, wooing us, and sending people to witness to us until we surrendered our lives to His will, His purposes, and His plans. Then our destiny once again became aligned with His desires recorded in His book. It may have taken us longer to get to the place which God designed for us, but we are here now, walking in His desire, His plan, and His purposes for our lives. We are serving, living, and standing in His perfect will for our lives. It certainly has been a journey.

The place where you are now may not look like where you want to be friend, but I encourage you to continue to walk, continue to live, and continue to place one foot in front of another. You will get to where God's perfect will captures your destiny and the two become one. Keep walking and seeking His will! We are in His book.

Layer Five ~ Day Five

Self-Esteem

Judges 6:14-15

"Then the Lord turned to him and said, 'Go in this might of yours, and you shall save Israel from the hand of the Midianites. Have I not sent you?' So he said to Him, 'O my Lord, how can I save Israel? Indeed my clan is the weakest in Manasseh, and I am the least in my father's house.'"

~Heart Caption~

What do you do when you feel like Gideon in the above Scripture? Gideon said that his father's house is the weakest family in the city, and he is too young, inexperienced, and afraid to save anyone. Has this been a cry of your heart to your Heavenly Father when you felt inadequate or incapable of carrying out the job, calling, or instructions given to you by God, due to your self-esteem? This was Gideon's plight.

Here is a synopsis of Gideon's story. The children of Israel did evil in the sight of the Lord, so the Lord delivered them into the hand of Midian for seven years. The children of Israel had a covenant promise from God that if they lived holy and upright before Him, He would bless them; this blessing included keeping them from their enemies. However, after Moses and Joshua were off the scene, the children of Israel went back to old habits of sin and turning away from God. Their backsliding behavior removed the umbrella protection of the Lord's mighty arm and favor over their lives and thus made them vulnerable to their enemy oppressor. Here is where we find Gideon.

The Midianites would raid the crops of the children of Israel and take their food from their fields. The children of Israel were so afraid of the Midianites that they were hiding in caves and did nothing out in the open so as to reveal themselves to their enemy. In fact, Scripture says that the Midianites would come up against the children of Israel in great numbers, such as locusts. Judges 6:5 says, *"For they would come up with their livestock and their tents, coming in as numerous as locusts; both they and their camels were without number; and they would enter the land to destroy it."*

In order to save as much food as he could, Gideon would thresh wheat inside a winepress. Under normal conditions, wheat is normally threshed in the open air, and wine was made in a winepress. Although Gideon voiced his fears and even his inadequacies, he did not allow his circumstances to remain the same. He did what he could to help his family, even if that meant doing what was no longer normal and doing it in an unconventional way. Gideon was approached by the angel of the Lord at the winepress, and he was addressed as a mighty man of valor. Why? Because that was how the Lord God saw Gideon. Gideon saw himself as small, fearful, and the least of his clan, but the angel of the Lord met him right where he was in the winepress and called him out of the winepress. God never leaves us as He finds us. His heart is to always transform us, no matter how long the transformation may take.

Gideon did make it out of the winepress, and he went on to fight the Midianites and the Amalekites and won great victories for his people. But it started by him hearing the encouragement from the angel of the Lord and coming into agreement with God about who He said he was and then being obedient.

~Focus Point~

What name has the Lord called you?

_____

_____

_____

_____

What encouragement has the Lord spoken to you?

_____

_____

_____

_____

What did you do with the name and the encouragement spoken to you?

_____

_____

_____

_____

Layer Five ~ Day Six

Self-Esteem

Romans 12:3
"For I say, through the grace given to me, to everyone who is among you, not to think of himself more highly than he ought to think, but to think soberly, as God has dealt to each one a measure of faith."

~Heart Caption~

When we really get to the heart of the matter, self-esteem is just that: the esteem, regard for, respect for, honor, reverence for, approval, appreciation, and admiration of oneself. As we do regard, respect, honor, reverence, approve, appreciate, and admire ourselves, and we should, let us do so "soberly" and thoughtfully, also considering Romans 12:1-2, *"I beseech you therefore, brethren, by the mercies of God, that ye present your bodies a living sacrifice, holy, acceptable to God, which is your reasonable service. And do not be conformed to this world, but be transformed by the renewing of your mind, that ye may prove what is that good and acceptable and perfect will of God."*

We as born-again believers are to continuously be a living sacrifice to the Lord our God. A living sacrifice is not to be consumed with one's self-identity nor so caught up with one's looks, body figure or other outward appearances, status in life, education, or any other values that we no longer want to present ourselves as honorable and living sacrifices to the Lord. We are also not to be consumed with and conformed to the culture of this world. Yet, the Apostle Paul begs us as Christians to be transformed to think outside of the box of the culture whose mindset is built on the world's way of thinking, acting, and always lending itself to pleasing oneself. We are to be continuously renewing our mind by the word of God through the presence of the Holy Spirit in our lives in order that we may prove the good, acceptable, and perfect will of God.

Yet, there is a balance in that we must also pursue a healthy mental, emotional, and physical lifestyle; this also is a part of presenting ourselves as a living sacrifice to and for our Lord. This is what will keep us healthy in mind, body, and heart and will allow us to take our focus off of ourselves, how we look, and how we sound and turn our hearts towards our Father, as a living sacrifice. We must desire wholeheartedly to be pleasing to God and pursuing His good, acceptable, and perfect will for our lives and the lives of our families.

Take the focus off of yourself. Stop allowing the enemy to turn your eyes upon yourself. You are beautiful – fearfully and wonderfully made. Pursue God and His presence and allow His word to erase the enemy's lies that try to convince you that you are covered with flaws. You are the daughter or son of the King!

Layer Five ~ Day Seven

Self-Esteem

Zephaniah 3:17
"The LORD your God in your midst, The Mighty One, will save; He will rejoice over you with gladness, He will quiet you with His love, He will rejoice over you with singing."

~Heart Caption~

I imagine a home where a family dwells. The mom, dad, and children are all enjoying each other's company, and all is well. The father is smiling and playing with the children, and laughter is a loud and joyful sound in the home. During the course of the evening, one child takes a leap and jumps as he has seen his brother and sister do, and he believes just as they did that he would fall to safety and then take another leap. However, when he falls, he hurts himself and begins to yell out to his parents. The father comes and begins to console his son. He first lays his eyes on his son to assess the damage, and then in his deep, strong, secure, and comforting fatherly voice, he begins to quiet the fearful, hurting child with his presence, his voice, and his love. The love beams from his body; it's almost like a tangible love that can be felt from father to child. He quiets his son with his love.

This is a picture of our Heavenly Father. In the sweet times of our lives, He is there, smiling over us, watching us, confirming us, and providing direction, favor, guidance, and support as a Father does. Yet in times when we have missed the mark and have fallen down, He is still there for us. We may not know how we missed the mark, how things got so bad, or how the situation became so unrecognizable, and yet we delayed crying out to our Heavenly Father. Sometimes, we delay crying out to Him because of guilt or out of shame. Perhaps we were looking at other's lives and how they were "doing life," and we thought we could do it as they were doing it, but we were mistaken. We cannot do life as others. We have to submit our lives to God and live our lives as directed by Him.

When we fall and we finally recognize that we need His help, we cry out to Him. Just like a good father, He is immediately there, calming us, soothing us, and comforting us with His tender love. His love showers over us like a downpour of rain that soothes us and refreshes us from the sweltering suns of life that beat down on us. Our Heavenly Father's love consoles us and quiets us. We come under the protection of His loving arms, His will, His direction, and His security. He really is a good, good Father, and He secures us with His love and protection. Our Father picks us up from the places in life where we have fallen, drawing us, holding us, and sustaining us in and by His love.

During these times of intimate fellowship with our heavenly Father while He is holding us, He begins to sing over us melodious songs of love that enrapture our hearts and cause His beloved to rest, sleep, and awaken refreshed and renewed. Friend, rest in the arms of your Father's love. Stop trying to do, pretend, measure up, look, and appear perfect and "put together." Allow our heavenly Father's love to surround you and sing you into a peaceful place *in Him*.

~Focus Point~

1 Decree and Declare
The Lord my God is with me. He is in my midst.
He rejoices over me and embraces me with His love.
I declare that the Lord God Almighty rejoices over me and
His joy surrounds me, sustains me, and gives me strength.

My heavenly Father sings over me with loud singing that I hear in my spirit.

What is the song of the Lord that you hear in your ears?

_____

_____

_____

_____

What do you want to say to the Father from your heart?

_____

_____

_____

_____

Layer Six ~ Shame, Rejection, and Guilt

Layer Six ~ Introduction

Shame, Rejection and Guilt

Shame will grab you by your neck and hold you up so high that your feet are off the ground, and you are no longer able to walk nor take a step. While this choke hold is cutting off your life's air, your vision becomes obscured. All the while rejection has you in hiding. The funny thing is that you're hiding from your true self, you've been rejected for so long that you don't recognize who you really are. Guilt finally comes in and places a mantle of darkness over you, over your heart and tries to cover your destiny as a shroud of darkness. But I say to you that the light of Christ's love pierces through these three tentacles that the enemy uses to wrap you in his fetters and chains. Jesus breaks every fetter and shatters every chain.

Layer Six ~ Day One

Shame

Isaiah 61:7
"Instead of your shame you shall have double honor, And instead of confusion they shall rejoice in their portion. Therefore in their land they shall possess double; Everlasting joy shall be theirs."

~Heart Caption~

Every single word of Isaiah chapter 61 pierces my soul to its very core. It grips my heart as it washes over me, cleansing me, renewing, and then refreshing me. The chapter itself is so loving and filled with the mercy of God. In fact, I have personally come to know and accept Isaiah 61 as the chapter of divine exchange. The first word in verse seven is the word "instead," which means "in its place." As I take a personal liberty with the text, this is how I read Isaiah 61:7 (paraphrased):

In the place of your shame (disgrace, embarrassment, & humiliation)
You shall have double honor.
Instead of confusion (mistake, misunderstandings & slip ups)
they shall rejoice in their portion.
Therefore, in their land they shall possess double;
Everlasting joy shall be theirs.

You may have experienced a place, a station in life, or a season where disgrace and embarrassment were your portion. Perhaps unlike your friends, you would never let yourself live it down. Your friends tried to encourage you by telling you things would get better, but because you felt this was your "lot" in life, you built a home in that station called shame and humiliation. You could never come up out of this place because it was home to you. It was more than familiar; it was your everyday stance. You saw yourself as not being worthy of love, let alone God's love. You did not feel loved, and because you did not love yourself, you were incapable of loving others. Although you hungered deeply to be loved, this feeling, this sense of worth eluded you. Perhaps you even attempted for many years to be accepted by others, but shame, confusion, and humiliation would always have the final word.

Dear friend, a divine exchange is available to you in Isaiah 61:7. In fact, Isaiah 61 is quoted below in its entirety. Please read it in its full context so that you can experience the same cleansing, renewal, and refreshing that is available to you. Read, study, and meditate on these verses. I pray that as you do, you will experience His divine exchange.

The Spirit of the Lord GOD is upon Me, Because the LORD has anointed Me
To preach good tidings to the poor; He has sent Me to heal the brokenhearted,
To proclaim liberty to the captives, And the opening of the prison to those who are bound;
To proclaim the acceptable year of the LORD, And the day of vengeance of our God;
To comfort all who mourn, To console those who mourn in Zion, To give them beauty for ashes, The oil of joy for mourning, The garment of praise for the spirit of heaviness;
That they may be called trees of righteousness, The planting of the LORD, that He may be glorified." And they shall rebuild the old ruins, They shall raise up the former desolations,
And they shall repair the ruined cities, The desolations of many generations.

Strangers shall stand and feed your flocks, And the sons of the foreigner
Shall be your plowmen and your vinedressers. But you shall be named the priests of the LORD,
They shall call you the servants of our God. You shall eat the riches of the Gentiles,
And in their glory you shall boast.
Instead of your shame you shall have double honor,
And instead of confusion they shall rejoice in their portion.
Therefore in their land they shall possess double; Everlasting joy shall be theirs.
"For I, the LORD, love justice; I hate robbery for burnt offering; I will direct their work in truth, And will make with them an everlasting covenant. Their descendants shall be known among the Gentiles, And their offspring among the people. All who see them shall acknowledge them, That they are the posterity whom the LORD has blessed."
I will greatly rejoice in the LORD, My soul shall be joyful in my God; for He has clothed me with the garments of salvation, He has covered me with the robe of righteousness, As a bridegroom decks himself with ornaments, And as a bride adorns herself with her jewels.
For as the earth brings forth its bud, as the garden causes the things that are sown in it to spring forth, so the Lord God will cause righteousness and praise to spring forth before all the nations.

~Focus Point~

Highlight the many times Isaiah 61 reveals the divine exchange (i.e., beauty for ashes). Once you have done so, write them out and make them personal to you. Specifically, write out the "ashes" of your life that you desire the Lord to make beautiful. Then make this a point of prayer.

For me, one of my favorite divine exchanges is <u>healing the brokenhearted, to proclaim liberty to the captives.</u> *"He has sent Me to heal the brokenhearted, to proclaim liberty to the captives."* I have spent many years mourning over a life of decisions and choices that proved to not be the best for me and my children. I did so out of ignorance and my own frailties in life such as unhealthy exposures, unhealthy boundaries, and deeply rooted self-esteem issues. However, the Lord's healing power can right and redeem many wrongs in our lives and bring about redemption and reconciliation to put us on the right track. It can have us experience levels of both healing and deliverance; where there once was sheer agony and mourning, now there is praise, beauty, glory, forgiveness, kindness, and overwhelming feelings of success in life. How? By divine exchange which brought about God's healing power in my life.

Now I live, I walk, and I talk in the healing power of God. This is a resting place for me. This is not a place I visit; I abide here in the presence of God. I have made room for Christ in my life, and He now abides in my life. You, too, can do the same. It will not be an overnight exchange; this is a process. Many people do not want to go through the process, so they opt out of the exchange. I learned the hard way that the process is not bad, if you humble yourself and surrender your heart to the Lord. He gets in the process with you. You are not alone; He abides with you.

Here is where you can begin. Write out the "ashes" of your life that you desire the Lord to make beautiful. Then make them a prayer point.

_____

_____

_____

_____

_____

Layer Six ~ Day Two

Shame

Matthew 26:31-35
"Then Jesus said to them, 'All of you will be made to stumble
because of Me this night, for it is written: 'I will strike the Shepherd,
And the sheep of the flock will be scattered.'
But after I have been raised, I will go before you to Galilee. Peter
answered and said to Him, 'Even if all are made to stumble because
of You, I will never be made to stumble.'
Jesus said to him, 'Assuredly, I say to you that this night, before the
rooster crows, you will deny Me three times.' Peter said to Him,
'Even if I have to die with You, I will not deny You!' And so said all
the disciples."

~Heart Caption~

Have you ever been in the place where you did something that
you thought you would never do? Have you ever said, "I will never
do that..."? I believe we all have something buried deep down in our
past where we have said, "I will never do that..." and then we did it.
Beloved, just as it is hard for you to bring up from your past the
incident that you were hoping no one would ever find out about, it is
just as hard for me to type about mine.

The Apostle Peter was a robust man. I am sure he had an air
of confidence about him, being a fisherman and provider for his
family. He was among the first to be called by Jesus, and as such he
had been with the Lord longer than most of the other disciples. Peter
was part of the inner circle of Jesus' friends along with James and
John. He would often accompany Jesus not only to places of prayer
but also intimate healing opportunities. Yet when great difficulty

revealed its head, when it appeared that Jesus needed Him the most, Peter denied Him. Although Peter was often the one disciple who would say and do things that appeared to be solely from a knee-jerk reaction, when he made the statement to Jesus that he would give his life for Him, Jesus responded. *"Assuredly, I say to you that this night, before the rooster crows, you will deny Me three times."* And it was so.

Matthew 26:69-75

Now Peter sat outside in the courtyard. And a servant girl came to him, saying, "You also were with Jesus of Galilee."
But he denied it before them all, saying, "I do not know what you are saying."
And when he had gone out to the gateway, another girl saw him and said to those who were there, "This fellow also was with Jesus of Nazareth."
But again he denied with an oath, "I do not know the Man!"
And a little later those who stood by came up and said to Peter, "Surely you also are one of them, for your speech betrays you."
Then he began to curse and swear, saying, "I do not know the Man!"
Immediately a rooster crowed. And Peter remembered the word of Jesus who had said to him, "Before the rooster crows, you will deny Me three times." So he went out and wept bitterly.

The Apostle Peter initially shrunk back in his faith and even spoke of "going fishing" again, in the mindset of returning to his old life. However, once you have been in the presence of the Lord, your life is forever changed, and so was the Apostle Peter's. Shame and regret tried their best to get a stronghold in his life, but just as Peter's public denial of the Lord was not enough to separate him from the love of God, neither is your incident, accident, or "public denial." Early on, Jesus said to Peter in Luke 22:31-32, "And the Lord said,

'Simon, Simon! Indeed, Satan has asked for you, that he may sift you as wheat. But I have prayed for you, that your faith should not fail.'"

Beloved, you have wept bitterly long enough. You have wept and worn the coat of shame long enough. Listen to me as I say to you: it is over. It is now complete. Jesus is standing before you, asking you the same questions that He asked Peter in John 21:15-17:

So when they had eaten breakfast, Jesus said to Simon
Peter, "Simon, son of Jonah, do you love Me more than these?"
He said to Him, "Yes, Lord; You know that I love You."
He said to him, "Feed My lambs."
He said to him again a second time, "Simon, son of Jonah, do you love Me?"
He said to Him, "Yes, Lord; You know that I love You."
He said to him, "Tend My sheep."
He said to him the third time, "Simon, son of Jonah, do you love Me?" Peter was grieved because He said to him the third time, "Do you love Me?"
And he said to Him, "Lord, You know all things; You know that I love You."

For each time of Peter's denial, Jesus met him at the point of his need, placing His finger on the very place of Peter's heart and breathing life and purpose into him. *"Peter, do you love Me?"* Jesus was drawing Peter in closer to Himself instead of pushing Him away, ignoring Him, and allowing Satan to get a foothold into his life.

Jesus knew that it was the Father's will to have Peter guide the apostles and the New Testament Church into the new beginnings they were on the forefront of experiencing, including trials and sufferings the Church would encounter. Peter would be at the head of this movement until he himself would be martyred for his faith, not the shame that he went through. It is believed that the Apostle Peter indeed was crucified just as his Lord; however, it is noted in some commentaries that Peter asked to be crucified upside down.

~Focus Point~

In His loving manner before He departed, Jesus restored Peter to his rightful place in Him. Just as Jesus restored Peter, my desire and prayer for you is that you, too, are restored in Christ. The shame of what you did, what you did not do, what you said, what you did not say, or even who you said it to, is all behind you now. Repent. Let it go. Release it from your being, and it will be relinquished from you. There is much work to do, and you are part of the work. Just as the Apostle Peter was part of the work of the Day of Pentecost, you are also a part of the next move of God. I submit to you the same questions with the same command Jesus gave to the Apostle Peter:

Beloved believer, do you love Jesus? Feed His lambs.
Beautiful believer, do you love Jesus? Tend to His sheep.
Beholden believer, do you love Jesus? Feed His sheep.

Layer Six ~ Day Three

Rejection

Isaiah 49:15-16

*"Can a woman forget her nursing child, And not have compassion
on the son of her womb?
Surely they may forget, yet I will not forget you. See, I have inscribed
you on the palms of My hands; Your walls are continually before
Me."*

~Heart Caption~

Zion, the endearing name given to the Church, cried out to the
Lord God in Isaiah 49:14 saying, *"But Zion said, The LORD has
forsaken me, and my Lord has forgotten me."* Have you ever said this
from the depths of your heart? Perhaps it revealed itself as a whisper
in the shadows of utter darkness. Maybe it was released from your lips
before you could rescind the thought. In the pages of Scripture, the
prophet Isaiah speaks openly what is often revealed in our hearts;
however, he never asked, "Has God forsaken and forgotten me?"

I have cried within my heart and with tears crisscrossing
underneath my chin, but I have never said those words. Not out of
shame, not even out of unbelief, but solely out of fear. If God has
forsaken me and if my God forgets me, who will help me? Where will
I go? There is no place where we, those who are deemed the people
of God can go; only He can help us. The Apostle Peter said it like this
in John 6:68, *"But Simon Peter answered Him, 'Lord, to whom shall
we go? You have the words of eternal life.'"*

Beloved, listen to what our heavenly Father says to us: "Can a woman forget her nursing child, and not have compassion on the son of her womb? Surely they may forget, yet I will not forget you. See, I have inscribed you on the palms of My hands; Your walls are continually before Me" (Isaiah 49:15-16). Friend, we are ever before the Lord our God. Our walls are before Him. He cannot forget us. Love never forgets the one whom He loves. Love does not forget the child He called forth from the mother's womb. Love remembers, love reminisces, love calls us into being and recalls, over and again, until divine alignment and fulfilment completely covers us as a crown upon our heads and a robe, a garment, a mantle upon our being. We are remembered, beloved. We are recalled to His mind. Love has not forsaken, abandoned, discarded, deserted, nor rejected us. Instead, He has taken up a holy habitation with us. His name is called Emmanuel – God with us. He is not just with us only during the Christmas season, friend. He is with us in our current situations, seasons, and all times throughout eternity. Do not believe the enemy's lies that remind us continuously of those who rejected or abandoned us in our times of need. No; our heavenly Father stepped into our lives, and He has remained. He has stayed in the fight with us, comforting, securing, and demonstrating His gentle mercy toward us, letting us know that He is with us and He has not forsaken nor forgotten us.

Beloved, our heavenly Father loves us immensely. He gave His only begotten Son for our life and the lives of all humanity – that is love. He has not abandoned you, me, nor humanity. We are engraved upon His hands and our walls are ever before Him.

~Focus Point~

Talk to your heavenly Father. It is only you and God; what do you wish to say to Him? Would you say that you feel lost and in need of the help that only He can provide? Imagine that there are two chairs in the room. You are sitting in one chair, and your heavenly Father is sitting in the other directly in front of you. He is relaxed and His eyes are gently fixed on you, a kind smile is on His face, and He is leaning forward towards you. He desires to be close to you. As He leans in your direction, He takes His right arm, reaches toward you, and rests His right arm and hand upon your hands in your lap. Do you feel the warmth of His touch and His presence?

Write what you want to say to your heavenly Father. He is listening.

_____

_____

_____

_____

_____

_____

_____

_____

Layer Six ~ Day Four

Rejection

Isaiah 49:16
"See, I have inscribed you on the palms of My hands; Your walls are continually before Me."

~Heart Caption~

Allow Me

I am a God who is involved in every detail of your life.
I am attentive to you and all who belong to you.
I love you My child, My son, My daughter.
You are Mine, and I have inscribed you upon the palms of My hands.
Have I not said that you are the apple of My eye?
Have I not placed My companions – goodness and mercy – to follow you all of your days?
Have I not said that your steps are ordered and that the entrance of My Word gives light?
Follow Me, My child. Follow Me in all of My ways.
Take no thought for your journey for My plans are sure.
Allow Me to lead you; allow Me to guide you.
Allow Me to love you and display My affections towards and upon you.
Allow Me to love you, My child, for surely, I do.

Layer Six ~ Day Five

Rejection

Hebrews 13:5
"Let your conduct be without covetousness; be content with such things as you have.
For He Himself has said, 'I will never leave you nor forsake you.'"

~Heart Caption~

God makes a bold declaration to His people: I will never leave you nor forsake you. Our heavenly Father makes this declaration to you and me today.

Perhaps if your earthly father did not live with you, you remember what it was like when he said that he would be by your house to pick you up at a certain time. With every car that sounded vaguely like your daddy's car, you looked in the direction of that car because you wanted it to be him coming to pick you up. When he did come, before he knocked on the door, you had already opened the front door and your eyes were wide with jubilant anticipation. You did not care what you and your dad did while you were with him, as long as you were together. The days of missing him, waiting on him, and him showing up only sometimes were nothing compared to those moments when you two were together.

Perhaps you have the same story, but maybe instead of you waiting on your dad, you were waiting on your mom, and she almost never showed up when she said she would. I know firsthand what it is to both leave and abandon someone I love – my child, my own flesh and blood. I have had to deal with the fact that I left and abandoned my oldest son due to my addiction to crack cocaine. What makes me feel the worst is the time I spent being away from him – him missing me and me missing him. There is so much time, involvement, and milestones in his life that I missed that I can never get back.

This makes this statement from our Lord Jesus Christ even more personal to me. Our Lord says to you that no matter where you may find yourself – in a vacant building, in a prison cell, on the island of Alcatraz, in an emotional graveyard afraid to come out, or in an emotional depressive state contemplating suicide. He will never leave you – NEVER! He will never loosen His grip on our lives. Sometimes we become so slippery with the challenges of life that you would think that we would slip past Him. Friend, that is when His grip gets tighter. It is tighter than the lie you told to your attorney, tighter than the lie you told to your wife or your boss. His grip becomes even tighter to hold us because He keeps His promises. He keeps His covenant. Even when we have given up on ourselves and do not have enough faith to walk past the guy or girl on the corner, He has us in His grip and His arms are tightly around us.

~Focus Point~

God says, "I will never leave you nor forsake you."

Beloved, take this time to write a love letter to the Lord. This letter is just for you and your heavenly Father. Write to Him thanking Him for never forsaking nor leaving you alone or behind. Thank Him that although you could not see it then, you see it now that He has always been there. Let Him know that in and through every turn, you now realize that He has been there all along. Thank Him for being there, staying there, and helping you to see and realize that He has never, nor will He ever, leave nor forsake you. Never!

Layer Six ~ Day Six

Guilt

Colossians 2:11-15

"In Him you were also circumcised with the circumcision made without hands, by putting off the body of the sins of the flesh, by the circumcision of Christ, buried with Him in baptism, in which you also were raised with Him through faith in the working of God, who raised Him from the dead. And you, being dead in your trespasses and the uncircumcision of your flesh, He has made alive together with Him, having forgiven you all trespasses, having wiped out the handwriting of requirements that was against us, which was contrary to us. And He has taken it out of the way, having nailed it to the cross. Having disarmed principalities and powers, He made a public spectacle of them, triumphing over them in it."

~Heart Caption~

Christ's ruling:
Not Guilty
Not Guilty
Not Guilty

All spiritual rulers and authorities in your life have been made a public spectacle that has been triumphed over by Christ! By your confession and personally applying Colossians 2:11-15 to your life, your trespasses have been forgiven, because the requirements that stood against you have been taken away; they've been nailed to the cross. You are not guilty, friend. There is a destiny that your heavenly Father has been calling you to. The enemy has tried your entire life to keep you from God's plan, God's destiny for you. However, now that you are aware of not only the enemy's plans of destruction for your life but also God's plan to give you a full, complete, and abundant life, it is even more important that you choose not to live your life with the conviction of "guilty" hanging over your head and looming over your life.

When you accepted Christ as your Lord and Savior, there was a spiritual transformation that took place. Colossians 1:13-14 says, *"He has delivered us from the power of darkness and conveyed us into the kingdom of the Son of His love, in whom we have redemption through His blood, the forgiveness of sins."* You, beloved, are now in the Kingdom of God's dear Son, Christ Jesus the Lord. Every former spiritual conviction, every spiritual ruling pronounced over your life by the spiritual rulers and authorities of the kingdom of darkness, has been overturned by Christ Jesus. Friend, your sins, my sins, and all of humanity's sins were nailed to Calvary's cross. Isaiah 53:4-7 (below) says it best.

~Focus Point~

Isaiah 53:4-7
Surely He has borne our griefs
And carried our sorrows;
Yet we esteemed Him stricken,
Smitten by God, and afflicted.
But He was wounded for our transgressions,
He was bruised for our iniquities;
The chastisement for our peace was upon Him,
And by His stripes we are healed.

All we like sheep have gone astray;
We have turned, every one, to his own way;
And the Lord has laid on Him the iniquity of us all.
He was oppressed and He was afflicted,
Yet He opened not His mouth;
He was led as a lamb to the slaughter,
And as a sheep before its shearers is silent,
So He opened not His mouth.

Friend, the reason Scripture boldly declares that you and I are not guilty of Satan's charges against us is because those charges were borne by Christ as He was crucified on Calvary's cross. Jesus paid the price for our sins. We are now adopted into the family of God. We are free and no longer guilty. Hallelujah! You are free in the Spirit of God. The former charges are now canceled, and you are no longer guilty. Hear the Lord Jesus saying that to you, whispering that in your ears. Listen to this personal declaration from Isaiah 53 (paraphrased):

You, beloved, are not guilty.
I took all your charges and I bore them in My body upon the cross.
My flesh was pierced for your rebellion.
I was crushed for your sins.
I was beaten so that you would be made whole.
I was whipped so that you would be healed.
I was oppressed and treated harshly for your peace.
I gave My life for you because I love you.
Choose to live your life in the victory I have provided.
Remember, you are no longer guilty – I've paid the price and you are now FREE.

Layer Six ~ Day Seven

Guilt

Romans 8:1

"There is therefore now no condemnation to those who are in Christ Jesus, who do not walk according to the flesh, but according to the Spirit."

~Heart Caption~

Beloved, remember the thing that you did that no one knew about but you? Every time it would come to your mind, stinging tears would flood your eyes and your lips and chin would begin to tremble – that thing. Remember how when you would think of it you felt all of the same feelings, you smelled the same smells of the building or the place, you even heard the music that was playing, if there was music playing, when everything was taking place? That thing. It hurt, and you asked yourself, "how did I get here?" No answer seems good enough, and yet the tears did not seem to be enough to express your sorrow, both for doing what you did and even for being caught for doing what you did. The hurt in your chest is reflective of the pain in your heart; how could I let this happen **again**? Yes, that thing.

I have worn those shoes before. I know what size they are. Those shoes are a "one size fits all" shoe. Everyone may not admit to being at that place, but deliverance is available for those who will admit it. To those who do – the Spirit of the Lord says to you *"There is now NO CONDEMNATION to those who are in Christ Jesus."* The key is *"to those who are in Christ Jesus."* That is the key. If you are in Christ Jesus, as the Apostle Paul wrote to the Romans, you are no longer condemned. You are a new creation in Christ Jesus and therefore Christ does not condemn you for everything that you have done and all that is *now* in your past.

The Apostle Paul speaks further in his exhortation, "who do not walk according to the flesh, but according to the Spirit." He gives us a direct lifeline to how we need to walk – not after the things of the flesh, our way, our will, and pleasing what our flesh cries out for. Now, place the flesh on the altar and allow the Holy Spirit to burn up those wants, desires, passions, and works of the flesh.

What are works of the flesh? Galatians 5:19-21 (paraphrased) notes the works of the flesh as such: *"Now the works of the flesh are manifest, which are these; Adultery, fornication (sexual intercourse with anyone outside of marriage), uncleanness (physical and morally unclean), lasciviousness (outrageous, shamelessness lust), Idolatry (worship of false gods), witchcraft (the use or administering of drugs, sorcery, magical arts), hatred (hostility, ill-will), variance (strife, contention), emulations (an envious and contentious rivalry), wrath (boiling with anger), strife (fighting, friction, trouble), seditions (disunity, bringing division), heresies (act of taking, capturing, storming a city), Envying (ill-will, provoked by jealousy), murders (killing or slaughtering), drunkenness (intoxication, drunk), reveling (riotous half-drunken person parading through the streets), and such like: of the which I tell you before, as I have also told you in time past, that they which do such things shall not inherit the kingdom of God."*

Galatians 5:22-25 (paraphrased) says: *"But the fruit of the Spirit is love, joy, peace, longsuffering (to suffer long), kindness (gentleness in dealing with others), goodness, faithfulness, gentleness, self-control (the virtue of one who masters his desires and passions, especially his sensuous appetite). Against such there is no law. And those who are Christ's have crucified the flesh with its passions and desires. **If we live in the Spirit, let us also walk in the Spirit.**"*

I testify to you that when you clothe yourself with Christ, walk in the Spirit, and come away from walking after your own desires and your flesh, you will walk yourself right out of barriers that have tried to control you and keep you bound to generational curses. Those things that your parents did that hurt you will no longer be prevalent in your life. Those things that your parents said or didn't say and the way they may have acted that hurt you and your family will not replay itself in your life.

Friend, walk in the Spirit. Put on Christ, just like you put on a brand-new suit. Put on Christ, and you will not fulfill the lust of the flesh. The word of God does not say that you would not feel lust, or fleshly desires; it says that you would not fulfill (achieve, accomplish, satisfy) the lust of the flesh. Will it be easy? No; nothing in this life worth achieving is easy. But how badly do you want it? Folks want a lot of things, but they are not ready or willing to work for them. Beloved, you do not have to work for salvation; it is a gift of God in Christ Jesus. However, to live a righteous and productive life, one that will produce fruit and keep you in a place where you are walking, thriving, and running in the Spirit, there will be the need for participation on your part. Nothing worth having will ever be given to you – except salvation!

Take hold of this promise: "There is therefore now no condemnation to those who are in Christ Jesus, who do not walk according to the flesh, but according to the Spirit." Let's walk together, boldly into the Kingdom of God and His promises for our lives!

A Final Word about Shame, Rejection, and Guilt

The coronavirus pandemic during 2020-2021 burned the following emotional proclivities from my life: approval addiction, people pleasing, self-rejection, and the high tolerance for emotional pain. Because I had a very high tolerance for emotional pain, you could say things to me and abuse me emotionally and I would <u>not</u> dismiss myself from your presence; I would take it. I had a very high tolerance for emotional abuse because I had, through the years, built up such a tolerance for it that it was almost like second nature. I also had a very high tolerance for bitterness and anger. I would not cut you off because I became bitter and/or angry with you. I would continue to remain your friend and chalk up the things that you said and did to me as a "me thing" – it was not about you, it was about me. I would say things like, "I'm too sensitive; I need to let that roll off my back," or, "He or she didn't mean that. They're angry. They have something else going on; it's not meant for me."

But during the pandemic, the Lord burned all of that out of my life. I was alone with my thoughts and had no one to "people please," no one to approve of me, and no one to be angry with or bitter against or even to be jealous of. I had no one to tolerate me, no one to exercise my pain with or have the tape recorder playing back in my ear over and over again. When I no longer had that, I had my soul and my spirit crying out to God.

The Holy Spirit said to me, "I want you in this time. I need you in this season. I have come to you specifically for this purpose, and I am allowing your alone time and your spiritual and emotional proclivities to be burned up in Me. I am creating the fire, and if you would be willing to cast off all of those things – the tentacles of the enemy and everything that has restrained you. If you would be willing to cast it all off, I will burn them up in My holy fire. When you look at it, it will look like wax that is melting off you. All of your emotional instabilities and those things that have stood as giants in your life will all melt like wax off of your life and off of your spirit. You have not been able to see your destiny because the mountains were so big, so large, so wide – you could not see your destiny around them. But if you would let My fire melt the mountain, melt those restraints, melt those cords of rejection, melt those cords of sadness, they will melt off of you like wax."

Remember the demon-possessed man from the country of the Gadarenes who was in chains and nothing and no one could hold him? But when Jesus saw him and spoke healing to his life, we later find him at the feet of Jesus in his right mind and peaceful. He was healed in his spirit, soul, and body. That is the kind of healing Jesus wants to bring to you. That is the kind of healing Jesus brought and continues to bring to me. That is the kind of healing Jesus wants to baptize us in. But we have to draw near; it only happens when we draw near. When we draw near, that is the physical, emotional, and spiritual evidence that we are ready to receive Him. Draw near to the Lord God and receive His healing. Receive that which He has for you so that He can cause those things that have held you back and have prevented you (emotionally, physically, and/or spiritually) to fall away. They will melt off of you like wax. They will literally melt in the presence of God.

Layer Seven ~ Fear

Layer Seven ~ Introduction

Fear

Say this with me: "Fear has held me back long enough!" Say it a few more times, then pause and give ample thought to what you have just decreed. Make it more personal by saying, "FEAR, you have held me back long enough!" If you believe that, how will it change the narrative of your life going forward? What will you do differently if FEAR was no longer one of your colleagues? I am not asking you about your finances, support, a building, a title, nor a platform; what would you do if FEAR was taken out of the equation? If you knew that God said to you, "I'm propelling you forward," what would you do first?

Layer Seven~ Day One

Fear

Genesis 3:9-10
"Then the LORD God called to Adam and said to him, 'Where are you?'
So he said, 'I heard Your voice in the garden, and I was afraid because I was naked; and I hid myself.'"

~Heart Caption~

In the book of Genesis, we find the first mention of the word fear. Some may have learned of the story of Adam, Eve, and the serpent in the Garden of Eden in Sunday school. This story has great ramifications for life as we take a closer look at what happened in the Garden, especially as it pertains to fear.

Eve was tricked by the serpent Satan into eating from the tree which God had instructed Adam not to eat of. The Scripture says that Eve ate, and she gave it to her husband who was with her, and he ate, too. Scripture also says that the moment they ate, their eyes were opened; they felt shame at their nakedness and sewed fig leaves to cover themselves. Then we see God walking in the cool breeze, and the man and the woman heard Him so they hid themselves among the trees. God called out to the man in Genesis 3:9-10: *"Then the Lord God called to Adam and said to him, 'Where are you?' So he said, 'I heard Your voice in the garden, and I was afraid because I was naked; and I hid myself.'"*

Adam became afraid of the only Father he had ever or would ever know – the Father who created him and created the universe and everything living, including his wife. He became afraid of his Father – the Father who made him in His image, gave him His mind and the ability to create. Up until that time, Adam and the Father took walks in the garden, and Adam knew His voice and His footsteps. How could Adam allow fear to come in and in an instant strip him of all that he possessed in God his Father?

It was not fear that stripped Adam of what was rightfully his; it was sin. Sin came into the garden in the form of disobedience, provoked by Satan stealing from Adam and Eve what God had given to them. From that day forward, God had to put a plan in place for redemption that would come through the generations of Abraham, Isaac, and Jacob and be born at such a time to redeem man's rightful place. What was the disobedient act? The first humans broke the rule that God had given them in Genesis 2:16-17: *"And the LORD God commanded the man, saying, 'Of every tree of the garden you may freely eat; but of the tree of the knowledge of good and evil you shall not eat, for in the day that you eat of it you shall surely die.'"*

Often, it is not what we are permitted to do but what we are not permitted to do that draws us into the line of suspense and the line of fire. Our cravings open up, and our senses begin desiring that which we cannot have. We, as human beings, have a will – the part of us which says I will do this, and I will not do that. It often gets us into trouble, especially after God gives us instructions of what to do: *"therefore choose life, that both you and your descendants may live"* (Deuteronomy 30:19b). Eve had a choice, and so did Adam. They both had a will and could have made the choice to obey God and live; however, they chose to gratify their flesh and disobey God. Because of this great error, mankind was thrust into the life where we are all born into sin and shaped in iniquity.

How does this have anything to do with fear? Adam was in a son's position, never wanting or needing anything. He and Eve had access to everything in the garden including the tree of knowledge of good and evil. A good father will always provide everything his family needs, including boundaries, instruction, and guidance. This is what God provided in the garden for His family: boundaries (you may eat of every other tree of the garden), instructions (but the tree of the knowledge of good and evil you shall not eat), and guidance (for in the day that you eat you shall surely die). Once Adam disobeyed his Father, he sinned. Now that Adam's eyes were open to good and evil, he knew that he and Eve were now naked, and they both felt shame. Their sin caused them to experience fear; they were now afraid of being seen by their Father who they previously had enjoyed a wonderful relationship with. Now they were afraid of Him. They were naked from the time that God formed them both and planted them in the garden and they had not been fearful. They had never felt fear until the act of disobedience was committed. Eve thought that she wanted to be wise and that she would know good and evil and be like her Father, so she took of the fruit and ate and gave to her husband who was with her.

Dear precious friend, Adam and Eve were made in the image of their Father, God. They had His likeness. They had spiritual likeness – spirit, soul and body. They had the mental likeness of their Father, for God commanded them in Genesis 1:28, *"Then God blessed them, and God said to them, "Be fruitful and multiply; fill the earth and subdue it; have dominion over the fish of the sea, over the birds of the air, and over every living thing that moves on the earth."* A person does not have dominion over something without the mental capacity to do so. Eve already had everything she needed to be the woman God called her to be, and Adam had all that he needed.

Friend, you are too great to be fearful! Adam and Eve were too great to be fearful. But they were tricked by the enemy into believing that they were not enough; they were tricked into believing that they did not have enough. Everything they needed was provided for them by their Father, God – everything. Yet that is where our problems lie most of the time, in us having conversations with the enemy, listening to the enemy of our soul, and then believing what Satan has said. The lie is that we are not enough, and we do not have enough. Friend, you are made in the image of God, and you have everything you need to move forward. You may not have everything you need to take step #10, but you do have everything you need to take step #2 if you are on step #1. Do the first thing first; you will get to all the steps you need to get to. I have had to learn that what is required for step #10 is what you will learn in taking steps #1-9, but you have to take those steps and complete them first. Do not allow the enemy to cause you to step over into unbelief, second-guessing, and disobedience; all of these are the tentacles of fear manifesting and showing up in your life in different ways. Remember, it was disobedience that caused Adam and Eve to end up in fear.

~Focus Point~

Fear no longer has a say so in your life. Fear no longer has a hold on you. You are no longer believing that you are not enough, nor that you do not have enough. You are made in the image of God, and you have all that you need.

Say this with me: Fear has held me back long enough!
FEAR has held me back long enough!

Once more: Fear, you have held me back long enough!
No longer, fear! You will not hold me back any longer!

Layer Seven~ Day Two

Fear

1 John 4:18
"There is no fear in love, but perfect love casts out fear.
because fear involves torment. But he who fears has not been made
perfect in love."

~Heart Caption~

Have you heard stories of people lifting cars off of their loved ones during times of great stress, panic, and even fear? How were they able to do that? I believe that it was not only due to adrenaline but also compassion for humanity, and in some personal cases, because of love. Because of their love for the individual who was afflicted and in extreme pain, the difficult feat before them caused them to not consider their own frailties or their own fears. They acted solely out of love and, in some cases, even neighbors acting out of humanity for another living, breathing soul, putting themselves in harm's way. Why? Because of the love of their child, a family member, a friend, or even a stranger. Fear would have held them back. However, their love overpowered any and all resistance in the form of fear and blocked its effects. That is just what love does. Love does not consider fear. Love does not have conversations with fear. Perfect love does not entertain fear.

The body of a soon-to-be mom is transformed over the process of nine months and becomes home to a growing, stretching baby. How is this mom able to endure the changes her body takes on? In most cases, it's because of love. When it is time for the baby to be born, the mother's entire body is transformed yet again, sometimes within hours; this is the most painful transition of all, known as the stages of labor. The mom endures what seems to be the most painful and stressful challenge upon their body that she has ever endured. Yet mothers do so, sometimes over and again, because of love. On the birthing table, the baby is in position after the bones in the mother's pelvis area have shifted, the cervix is finally dilated the full 10 centimeters, and with the nurses' and doctor's approval, the mother is urged to push and breathe, breathe and push. The mother gives one final, exhaustive push, and the baby that once was within is now taking his or her breathe for the first time outside of the womb. Through the excruciating pain of deliverance, the mother gives birth by love. The love perfected in the mother for the baby she is giving birth to causes her to not react in fear, but she does all she can to deliver her baby because of love. Fear would try to prevent her from doing so, but her love does not give way to fear. Her love for her baby, especially in the womb, strengthens her to cover and shield her baby until she has pushed her baby into her and the father's loving arms. Love allows her to endure. Love graces her to endure the pain of pregnancy and childbirth and enraptures her for the next season of the child's life. Love does all of this, without even considering fear.

Scripture says of Jesus *"…who for the joy that was set before Him endured the cross, despising the shame…" (Hebrews 12:2b)*. How did Jesus Christ endure the cross? The joy set before Him. How did those family members who endured hurt and debilitating circumstances to save a loved one from tragedy endure the challenge of car wrecks and other debilitating circumstances? The joy of the safety and well-being of their family member or friend set before them. What about the mom of the newborn, delivering the baby in the most painful crisis she may ever experience in life? The joy of her beautiful baby set before her. Beloved, we are Christ's joy. We are Christ's crown. We are Christ's royal diadem. We are Christ's beloved bride.

~Focus Point~

Friend, you are Christ's joy, His prized possession. His love for you is always at the forefront of everything He sees and all that He has planned for you. His love is perfected towards you. There is no fear in Him. Let there no longer be any fear in you. Let Christ's love rule in your hearts and perfect you, your heart, and your mind so that fear will no longer have a stronghold. As Christ's love rises in your heart, a new courage and boldness will arise and be ever present in your life. Friend, perfect love casts out fear. Be perfected in love. Love strong and love hard for this same love was exemplified in Christ upon Calvary's cross. For the joy of all of humanity that was set before Him, He endured the cross, despising the shame and is now sitting at the right hand of the throne of God.

For the joy of (insert your name and the names of your family members here)

_____

_____

_____

_____

set before Him, Christ endured the cross despising the shame and is now sitting at the right hand of the throne of God.

Layer Seven ~ Day Three

Fear

Psalm 56:3-4

"Whenever I am afraid, I will trust in You.
In God (I will praise His word), In God I have put my trust;
I will not fear. What can flesh do to me?"

~Heart Caption~

All of us will face a day or perhaps even seasons in our lives when we are afraid, where our hearts are disturbed and overwhelmed with fear and intimidation. In such times, we do not know what to do or say. Our words seem to escape us. During these seasons of great distress where our hearts are fainting because of the fear that has overtaken us, we may find it hard or extremely difficult to trust anyone. We become suspect of everyone. This is what fear does – it places us in a space where we feel we have lost control of our present situation, our previous plans have failed, and therefore, we are without hope.

The sweet psalmist of Israel, as bold and courageous as he was, proclaimed in Psalm 56:3, *"Whenever I am afraid, I will trust in you."* Friend, we all will have a day when we are afraid. We may face the loss of a dear family member, the disturbing news from a doctor's report, the loss of a job, the loss of a home, or the loss of one's freedom due to prison. Especially with the world undergoing the season of COVID-19, we have all experienced severe loss and desperate situations of fear. However, regardless of the reason for our fears, the Lord is speaking to us and imploring us to invite Him in.

The psalmist David said, *"In God I have put my trust; I will not fear."* He learned to trust in the Lord and not in himself. Through this posture of heart in trusting God, David learned to invite the Lord into his circumstances, which provided an opening for him to lay all of his fears before the Lord. We carry what the Lord has instructed and commanded us to lay before Him. We do so by implementing 1 Peter 5:7, *"casting all your care upon Him, for He cares for you,"* and Philippians 4:6, *"Be anxious for nothing, but in everything by prayer and supplication, with thanksgiving, let your requests be made known to God."*

Friend, did you know that worry, fretting, and anxiety are all rooted in and manifestations of fear? What are you faced with today? Cast your care upon the Lord. The word cast means to throw upon or place upon. In prayer, we cast (throw upon, place upon) the Lord our cares, our concerns for family, friends, situations, circumstances, our nation, and our leaders, as we are commanded to do so according to 1 Timothy 2:2. We do all this in and through prayer.

Prayer is not only talking to the Lord, but prayer is also listening to the Lord. When you communicate, there is an exchange between one or more persons. When you communicate with the Lord in prayer, expect a divine response, though this response may not be audible. The Lord's response may be a slight or deep impression. His divine response may also be revealed in His Word. There are many other ways that the Lord may choose to speak to you: in dreams, through another person, or perhaps in a song. Nevertheless, do not limit His response to you. Be patient in speaking with Him and receiving from Him. We often want the results of His divine presence, but we often do not want to do what it takes to receive His divine presence. Wait on the Lord; do not be in a hurry to hear from Him. I have found that this is where the enemy will often rear his head – he will meet you in your "quick" desire for an answer. The Lord rarely does things in a hurry; however, He is always on time and never late.

Choose to trust God, friend. Choose to believe and wait upon the Lord. This will build your strength in Him, and you will see fear and anxiety dissipate. Fear will no longer have a settling place within you because you have made the Lord your trust.

~Focus Point~

Begin now to cast your cares upon the Lord. Begin by writing the fears that have held you back below. Tell God of the fears that have prevented you from trusting in Him and His Word. Make it a habit to go back and re-read what you have written, and then watch for His ways of speaking to your heart in unique ways. It will encourage you as you journey on to know the Lord.

_____

_____

_____

_____

_____

_____

_____

_____

Layer Seven ~ Day Four

Fear

Deuteronomy 31:6
"Be strong and of good courage, do not fear nor be afraid of them;
for the LORD your God, He is the One who goes with you.
He will not leave you nor forsake you."

~Heart Caption~

Stepping out into the known, and even more so the unknown, can be quite fearful or even dreadful. But when the Lord goes before you and He tells you that He is with you, you have nothing to fear.

In venturing off into the unknown, the children of Israel were about to lose their leader, Moses, and embark upon and establish a new leader, Joshua. Not only were they experiencing the "changing of the guard," but they were also venturing into new territory. They were coming up on their promised land.

The children of Israel had only known slavery, bondage, and the Egyptian Pharaohs for 430 years. Born into slavery and into bondage where you only heard stories of the mighty acts of the God your ancestors served, it must have sounded like fables to them as they had never seen these acts until Moses. When God heard the cry of the children of Israel, He raised up a deliverer in Moses. Although it took some time before Moses was moving forward in his calling, it was the right time for the children of Israel. Yet through all that they had watched Moses accomplish, they were now being informed that he would no longer be leading them and that God had chosen another leader. They had finally grown to trust Moses and the God of Moses, and although they were not perfect, they looked to Moses to be perfect for them, even to face God for them. Now that was being taken away from them.

Beloved, there are times in our lives when God strips away the first so that He can establish the second. As He does so, He gently whispers to us, "Do not be afraid. You are on the verge of accomplishing all that I have placed in your hands to do. Do not be afraid. I am going before you into this new and beautiful land, do not be afraid. I have placed a 'Joshua' before you, and although he is not what you were used to, I have called him. I am going before him, and I am instructing him. Do not be afraid."

Friend, just as the children of Israel were moving into their promised land, we, too, are moving into our new territories, our new promised lands. We are branching out, we are stretching forth, and God is still saying to us, "I know that you have not been this way before. You have not seen this before, and you have never felt this before. It is okay, I am going before you. Do not be afraid."

Receiving Jesus Christ as Lord of your life may be new. You may have never seen a Bible, let alone heard a hymn or a Christian song. Know and believe that the Lord our God goes before you and you have nothing to fear. You may not know, recognize, or see every turn, but here is where trust comes in. Trust the Lord to do just as He has promised that He would do. He will go before you, just as He said.

After the Covid-19 pandemic, the world is facing a new normal. How are we to handle this part of our lives? We will handle this part of our lives with the Lord our God going before us and not being afraid. He knows the end from the beginning. The Lord our God, the almighty sovereign one, is with us. He is our heavenly Father; we have nothing to fear. Take a step, move forward, and allow the Lord to go before you. He has promised that He will never leave you nor forsake you. It is all in His care. We are all in His care. Move forward without fear or hesitation, friend. He has covered your path, and nothing can stand before our God.

~Focus Point~

Write down some new things you are seeing and experiencing in your life that may be fearful to you. Write how you feel about them, your response to them, and how you believe the Lord would have you pray about them.

_____

_____

_____

_____

Layer Seven ~ Day Five

Fear

Psalm 27:1
"The LORD is my light and my salvation; whom shall I fear?
The LORD is the strength of my life; of whom shall I be afraid?"

~Heart Caption~

Have you ever been in a dark room that does not have windows, outside light, or anything that would bring in light except for the door to the room? The room is so dark that even after remaining in the room for several minutes, your eyes make no adjustment to the darkness. There are no shadows, for the blackness of the room now surrounds you and engulfs you. The darkness moves from a place of "seen" darkness to the place of "felt" darkness because of how tangible it has become; it seems that you could reach out and touch the darkness. However, were you to strike a match or turn on your phone, illumination would immediately permeate and infiltrate the room.

David said "the Lord is my light." God is the light that it takes to dispel the darkness in our lives. The Lord comes in and what appeared to be hopeless, dark, and impenetrable begins to break forth in light. John 1:4-5 states about God's light, *"In Him was life, and the life was the light of men. And the light shines in the darkness, and the darkness did not comprehend it."* The Lord Jesus still shines, friend. He shines on good days, but I have found that He shines brightest on bad days. God specializes in things that seem absolutely impossible to us. Recall all that David had faced; in everything that he went through, he learned to say, not from what he heard, but from his own experience, "The Lord is my light and my salvation, my rescuer in times of trouble." With this same statement and in this same breath, he states *"Whom shall I fear?"* He goes on to declare, *"The Lord is the strength of my life; of whom shall I be afraid?"*

~Focus Point~

In this one verse, David decreed and declared to himself over two thousand years ago a truth that as we live life in our current times with everything we are faced with, we can trust and place our beginnings and our ends in the hands of our heavenly Father. He is our light and our salvation and the strength, the fortress, the rescuer of our life; whom shall we fear?

Layer Six ~ Day Six

Fear

Isaiah 41:13
*"For I, the LORD your God, will hold your right hand,
Saying to you, 'Fear not, I will help you.'"*

~Heart Caption~

A story was told of a grandfather who was walking his grandchild from the corner ice cream store in a Bronx, New York neighborhood. The street gangs were prevalent in the neighborhoods at that time, and the streets were relatively unsafe. As the grandfather continued to walk the grandchild down the street to their home, they noticed some gang members approaching them. Once the grandchild noticed the gang members walking towards them, he stopped licking his ice cream cone and began watching the gang members in fear. He saw how big and hostile the gang members were, and he noticed them joking with one another and hearing them use extreme foul language. This made the child even more fearful so that he began to hold his grandfather's hand tighter as the gang members drew closer.

As they drew near to the gang members, the little boy heard his grandfather say: "Son, you know I love you, right?"

The child said, "Yes."

The grandfather said, "You know that I will let nothing happen to you, right?"

The child said, "Yes."

The grandfather said finally, "You know you have nothing to fear, right?"

The child hesitated but then thought about who his grandfather was and then he said, "Yes!"

The exchange reached both the heart and mind of the child so that he began to lick his ice cream cone in happiness once again. The child even began to skip because he was assured and reassured of who his grandfather was, that he was loved, and that he was holding the safe and loving hand of his grandfather.

~Focus Point~

Fearful things in life may have recently visited you in a very real and dramatic way. It may have walked down your street and even knocked on your door. I can only imagine your fear, hurt, and maybe disbelief, but just as the grandfather said to his grandson, I say to you:
"You know your heavenly Father loves you, right?"
"You know your heavenly Father will not let anything happen to you, right?"
"You know you have nothing to fear, right?"

Write your response to these questions here:

_____

_____

_____

_____

_____

_____

Layer Seven ~ Day Seven

Fear

Mark 5:36

"As soon as Jesus heard the word that was spoken, He said to the ruler of the synagogue, 'Do not be afraid; only believe.'"

~Heart Caption~

Crowds of people followed Jesus. Everywhere He went, He could barely move because of them. The more miracles He performed, the more people heard about Him and the more people followed Him. This day was no different. He had arrived by boat, and a large crowd had gathered around Him to see the next miracle He would perform. However, a synagogue ruler named Jairus was a part of the crowd that met Jesus. It is clear that Jairus believed that Jesus was the Son of God and the miracles which He performed were from God because when he saw Jesus, he fell at His feet and begged Him to come and lay His hands on his daughter who was dying. Jesus went with Jairus, and so did the crowd of people. While they were on their way, a woman with an issue of blood came up behind Jesus, pressing her way through the crowds of people, she touched Him. According to Mark 5:28, the woman said, *"If only I may touch His clothes, I shall be made well."* Even though Jesus, Jairus, and the crowd were still on their way to Jairus' home, Jesus felt a virtue of healing released from His body and He stood still, in the middle of the crowd and asked, *"Who touched My clothes?"* (Mark 5:30). The disciples wondered how Jesus could ask who touched Him when there was such a large crowd following them. While He was looking around to identify the person, she came forward, fell down before Him, and confessed. When she did, Jesus said to her *"Daughter, your faith has made you well. Go in peace, and be healed of your affliction"* (Mark 5:34). While Jesus was still speaking to the woman, Jairus' servants came to him in the crowd and brought him the news that his daughter was now dead; no need to bother the teacher. Jesus overheard what was said and spoke directly to Jairus saying, *"Do not be afraid, only believe"* (Mark 5:36).

Beloved, your life may very well have been impacted by crowds and disruptions that have followed and prevented you from moving forward. These crowds and disruptions may look like a broken home, a mother on drugs, a father or brother who verbally abused you, or a husband or high school boyfriend who physically abused you. It could have been a bully in middle school that never left you alone, or it was the rape in your college years that you never told anyone about. Perhaps it was the lie, told by your best friend, that landed you in jail, and now you are serving time for a crime someone else did.

~Focus Point~

Friend, our lives are overwhelmingly crowded with things that have happened to us that have caused disruptions in our mental and emotional lives. These may have even caused delays to the point that instead of moving forward, you were actually moving in circles over and over again until something so very precious within you died. You may be thinking that your destiny, the life you wanted to live, the life you planned to live, or the person who you planned to live it with are now dead. Beloved, hear the heavenly Father say to you *"Don't be afraid; only believe."* I know it may look bad right now, but Jairus still had a distance to go, even with the crowd, before Jesus got to his daughter to speak life back into her very being. When Jesus got there, He dispelled the darkness of those who did not believe and He took the child by the hand and said to her *"Little girl, _____* (put your name and your situation here), *I tell you to get up!"*

 Beloved, just as Jesus assured Jairus to not be fearful but only believe, take this very personal word and receive it for yourself. This man had several things stacked against him, just as you may have. He had the crowd that was preventing Jesus from moving as quickly as possible to get to his daughter. Then there was the situation with the woman which added more time, and then there was the final news that all was lost – the girl, his daughter, your daughter, is dead.

 Friend, all is not lost for you nor with you. Jesus is still saying, "Don't fear; only believe." No matter the delay of the crowd, no matter the circumstances or situations that have come up that provided even more of a hindrance or a blockage to your way; don't fear, just believe. All things are possible to you if you believe. Jesus loves to turn impossible things around, and He loves to raise dead things to life. It was the Lord's will to raise Jairus' daughter, and if it's His will to raise situations, circumstances, and dreams in your life, He will do so for you if you will only believe.

Layer Eight ~ Perfect Pride

Layer Eight ~ Introduction

Perfect Pride

Pride can be very tricky. When you have challenges or struggle with low self-worth or low self-esteem, over the course of time, you tend to find your value in the things that you do – especially if you've become very good at them. **Your work becomes your worth**.

Layer Eight ~ Day One

Perfect Pride

1 Corinthians 13:4
"Love suffers long and is kind; love does not envy;
love does not parade itself, is not puffed up."

~Heart Caption~

Love is the emblem of Christianity. It is because of love that God gave us His Son so that we would have life everlasting. The Son gave His life on the cross of Calvary. Have you ever thought about what held Jesus to the cross? Was it the nails? No, it was love. The love He has for you and me held Him to the cross. What a wonderful sacrifice and what an amazing display and example of love! Christ is love, and He draws us to Himself by His love. This is the kind of love that suffers long and is kind; this is the kind of love that does not envy nor parade itself and is not puffed up. This is the kind of love that says, "I will not accept the easy way out concerning you, nor humanity." Love says, "I am willing to sacrifice My all for you, for humanity."

According to C. S. Lewis, there are four unique forms of love that the Bible speaks of: (1) eros – erotic love, (2) storge – family love that develops between parents and children, (3) philia love – meaning dear one, friend, beloved, etc. and is expressed in friendships; and (4) agape, which is the term that we see in 1 Corinthians 13. It is noted as the highest form of love and describes the unconditional love of God, proven in the sacrificial love of Jesus Christ, and experienced purely through the Holy Spirit.

All forms of love are beautiful to behold, experience, and share along the journey of life. In fact, during one's lifetime, it is hoped that all four unique forms of love would be experienced. Yet there are two forms of love which we all can experience: philia love and agape love. The form of love known as philia has been expressed in the pages of this entire devotional. Every time that I say, "friend," "beloved," or "precious one," I am expressing philia love – expressions of love particularly in friendships. All of these forms of love can be experienced and demonstrated from a Biblical perspective; however we will focus on agape love. Agape love is noted as the highest form of love. Christ said in John 13:35, *"By this all will know that you are My disciples, if you have love for one another."*

Agape love gives the believer in Christ the internal and supernatural ability to love as Christ loves – withholding nothing, selflessly and sacrificially loving a person without exalting yourself or drawing attention to yourself by bragging about what you have done for the other person or exalting yourself or your efforts towards the person in any manner. This form of love is expressed as not being envious, not self-seeking, and not prideful. This form of love is always seeking the best and highest good for the other person, whether they are aware of it or not.

If one is to partake in the highest form of love, one must be willing to love generously without the focus being on themselves. As love is imparted into your life, if nurtured correctly, it will blossom and grow inwardly and then is manifested and displayed outwardly. You cannot hide love when it is real and true. It leaks out of you and runs to the driest place within another person to help, soothe, and quench the thirst of another. Love takes one beyond themselves and lifts one up for the better, never to destroy. In fact, love is seen and literally on display in the good times, however the heightened effect of love is at its best in the difficult times.

~Focus Point~

I had to learn that love is not only an emotion; love is also an action performed continuously, much like a decision that you are committed to time and time again. The commitment remains during the bad, the not so bad, the good, and the not so good times. I have found that, like me, people have to be taught, be exposed to, and experience waves and measures of Christ's love in order for them to truly love themselves, and then to share and give out of the abundance of their own storage of love to others. Without one truly being loved and experiencing agape love, one cannot give or share this purest form of love, no matter how hard one tries. In its truest form, love is so easy to do, share, and sit in. If you find it hard to love, it's probably not agape love.

Have you experienced agape love? Recall your experience. Thank and praise God for it, and then ask God for the opportunity to display love on this level to someone else.

_____

_____

_____

_____

Layer Eight ~ Day Two

Perfect Pride

1 Peter 5:5
*"Likewise you younger people, submit yourselves to your elders.
Yes, all of you be submissive to one another, and be clothed with
humility, for
'God resists the proud,
But gives grace to the humble.'"*

~Heart Caption~

Have you ever experienced the Scriptures in such a real and pure way where it seems like the words jump off the page? Here is one such instance for me. The Word of God talks to those "younger" in age a lot, specifically in Proverbs; however, 1 Peter 5:5 above is one of those places in the New Testament where it addresses those who are "younger" in the congregation with kind wisdom. Although I cannot judge or speak of every young person on the planet, it has been my experience that those who are younger in age are more frequently less likely to surrender or yield to their elders. I have noticed, specifically in this day and the culture in which we live, that young people tend to believe that they know more than adults. Technologically, this may be true. However, I have found that those of younger age are less tolerant of receiving advice from adults and even less likely to sit and be still to recognize the advice needed.

I say this not to discredit anyone but only to expose that I was exactly like this as a young person. I would not listen to anyone – my elders, neighbors, family, or friends. I was bent on doing things my way, not realizing that my hardheadedness, recklessness, and selfishness would result in decisions down the line that I would have to learn from and pay for.

As I matured and began to see the fruit of decisions I made, I began making this statement quite often: if only I had had someone in my life who had loved me enough to say, "Stop; you're going the wrong way. You're doing the wrong thing, and that decision will have consequences." Maybe if there was someone who would have helped me to see that just like right decisions are life-changing and long lasting, so are wrong decisions. Wrong decisions are also life-changing and long lasting. Unfortunately, due to my home environment, those words may have been said, mentioned, yelled, or screamed, but I didn't trust the advice coming from those in my house.

What would I say to young people today, given the opportunity? If you recognize that you have good, sound, godly parents, look to your parents. Loving, kind, sound, and godly parents are ones that embody love, care, and wisdom for you and have your best interest at heart. Your parents have sacrificed, and will continue, to make sure that you have all that you need – they should be your first go-to person for counsel and guidance. In the case that this may not be so for you, look for an elder (an adult), not one of your peers. Pray and ask the Lord to open your heart to the right mentor in an adult. This person should be one you respect, one who would be honest and transparent with you, and yet bold and courageous to share with you hard things that you may not want to hear but you need to hear. Look for this person in your local school, in your church, or in your neighborhood if you've been in your neighborhood for a number of years and have seen the honesty and wisdom of that person whom you wish to learn from and grow with. You need someone to whom you can submit. One thing for sure, if you have learned to submit to your parents, submission will not be different or difficult; yet some young people have not respected their parents to submit to them, and thus they have no respect for almost anyone in authority.

I say this to you in love: there is a grace that comes upon your life from the Lord when you humble yourself, putting yourself in a place where you allow yourself to be subjected to those in authority by yielding and submitting to them. The wonderful thing about being submitted is that it is not a young or old "thing." In fact, Ephesians 5:21 says, *"Submitting to one another in the fear of God."* A great way to look at this, especially if you are an older adult, is if you need help from your grandchild to help you understand your computer, tablet, or latest cell phone. It takes you as the adult to be subject to your grandchild; even though you're the adult, you look to the grandchild for advice and instruction in this particular area, and you listen and adhere in gentleness.

If you are a young believer, often you may feel and experience some resistance in your life because you have made your own way hard. You've moved everyone out of your life because of your hardness and more than likely your rebellion. As you are obedient to the Word of God and your heart is humbled, God's grace will begin to overshadow your life. Opportunities that previously eluded you will begin to open up for you. Ways are now being made for you. Why? Because the grace of God is now working for you. Continue to humble yourself. Listen to your elders. Don't be so quick to talk over them. You need what they have. It may not look like your peers' situations. Silver in the eyes of a child always looks like something that is just "shiny." However, there is great wealth in the silver flowing from the elder's mouth, and the experiences that they are willing to share with you will help you to grow, develop, and move ahead in life.

Listen, young king, young queen. Listen to your elders.
Just as the Scripture says, 1 Peter 5:5, "Likewise you younger
people, submit yourselves to your elders. Yes, all of you be
submissive to one another, and be clothed with humility, for 'God
resists the proud, But gives grace to the humble.'"

Layer Eight ~ Day Three

Perfect Pride

~Heart Caption~

Have you ever experienced a person who has built a room of hurt and disappointment that was walled so high and the bricks so thick that he/she could not let anyone in nor themselves out? They had been let down so much in life by those whom they had looked to and depended upon. Perhaps they were even abandoned so much that in order for them to mentally and/or physically survive, they had to put all their trust in themselves. This is a very lonely place to be – the place where you trust no one and you only believe in yourself because you know you won't ever let yourself down. Yet many of us have grown up with this frame of mind, and the enemy of our souls has used it to allow pride to creep in. We didn't readily see it as pride. In fact, if anyone would have said it was pride, we would have denounced it fully. However, often when subtle emotions such as pride slip in, they do so quite unaware until it is out of control and someone is yelling at us, saying, "Check yourself before you wreck yourself." All the while we swear that we are not being prideful; but who would admit to being prideful anyway?

Humbling oneself can be so humbling. Yet we are encouraged to do so on our own before God does it for us. I have found that one of the best ways that we can humble ourselves is to simply ask for help. Don't get caught up in your accomplishments, what you know, who you know, how much you have, or how much you used to have; simply ask for help. Another way of humbling yourself is to admit when you've missed it or gotten it wrong. For a lot of us, to say the words, "I was wrong" is almost like ordering a firing squad on ourselves. Precious one, this is simply humbling yourself under the mighty hand of God.

What comes after humbling oneself? Time; not God exalting you. Believe it or not, God's exaltation comes after time, and His timing is perfect. He allows time to show the person the beautiful place of humility and the ugly jungle of pride. God knows that often if one is exalted too quickly, pride comes on the heels of that exaltation. As the old mothers of the church used to say, "Stay low, child. Stay low."

Layer Eight ~ Day Four

Perfect Pride

Proverbs 22:4
"By humility and the fear of the LORD Are riches, and honor and life."

~Heart Caption~

How do you really feel about God? Before you answer, think about who you're really speaking of. Here are some things to think about before you answer.

"In the beginning God created the heavens and the earth" (Genesis 1:1). God has no creator. God has no beginning nor an end. He opens His book by displaying His creation. He created the sun, moon, stars, mountains, oceans, and land that we see. He created all animals, great and small. God created you and me in His image. God says about His Son, Jesus, *"In the beginning was the Word, and the Word was with God, and the Word was God. He was in the beginning with God. All things were made through Him, and without Him nothing was made that was made"* (John 1:1-3).

Friend, this is our God. Again, how do you really feel about God? Do you have awe and reverence for God? Our God is good, but there are so many other beautiful ways to describe Him that lead you into praise and reverential fear of who He is. Our God is majestic, all-powerful, holy, righteous, awesome, and sovereign over all things. He is the keeper when you want to be kept. He is the good shepherd, and He is the God of heaven's armies of angels. In the book of Exodus,

Moses exclaimed *"Who is like You, O LORD, among the gods? Who is like You, glorious in holiness, fearful in praises, doing wonders?"* (Exodus 15:11). Moses and the children of Israel penned this song and sang it after God split the Red Sea and the Israelites marched to safety on dry ground.

Beloved, this God is the one whom we worship, sing to, and give our lives to. This is our God! Because of who He is, we stand in awe of Him. We recognize His majesty and our finiteness in comparison to His infinite greatness! This is where our reverential fear comes from. Our hope, trust, and love keep us humbled and postured at His feet. Friend, no one else holds the keys to death, hell, and the grave except the Lord Jesus Christ. There is no man on planet earth, there never has been and never will be, who is able to stand in the presence of Jehovah God. This is the One to whom we owe our lives. In this life, you may have riches or acquire honor, but at the end of your life, where do you stand? The way to acquire true and everlasting riches and honor is by being humble and remaining in a posture of reverential fear of the Lord.

Over time, I have seen many people step out of this posture because it seems that they have gotten away with sin. They may have done something that was wrong to their fellow man or perhaps have said something wrong to another person and thought that the Lord God did not hear the complaints of their heart. Friend, when you walk in a place of humility, your entire life exemplifies humility. The Lord rewards and honors His servants – those who have remained in the place of humility by rewarding their life.

Precious one, life goes by so very quickly. In Christ, your life can be lived in victory when your heart belongs to the King of Kings and the Lord of Lords. However, some choose riches in this life instead of the richest of Christ's glory eternally. Make the heavenly choice now. As you kneel at the feet of Jesus when your life has ended, you will be so very thankful that you did.

~Focus Point~

Perhaps this is the only layer that you have read in this devotional, and upon reading it, you would like to make the Lord Jesus Christ your savior eternally. Or perhaps you would like to renew your commitment to Jesus as your savior. If so, please say this prayer with me.

Dear Jesus,
I am a sinner, and I have tried to be the captain of my life far too long. Thank You for loving me and sending Your only begotten Son to die for me so that I would have eternal life. Jesus, thank You for laying down Your life to save mine. I admit that I've made mistakes. I pray that You would save me and transform me. I now receive and accept You as my Lord and Savior. Amen

---

Name/Date

Layer Eight ~ Day Five

Perfect Pride

Romans 12:3
"For I say, through the grace given to me, to everyone who is among you, not to think of himself more highly than he ought to think, but to think soberly, as God has dealt to each one a measure of faith."

~Heart Caption~

I used to think that if I didn't do the work required by my boss, it would not get done. I also used to think that if I didn't perform certain work in my church, it would not get done. The pride of these thoughts was that I was the only person who could do the job. Yet in holding to this form of pride, I also suffered because I often did not ask for help. In other scenarios, especially regarding church and areas where community involvement was needed, I hindered others from using their talents and skills and providing their own pieces to the puzzle.

Lesson number 1: Everyone can play; you're not the only one who can fix a puzzle. It amazes me at how much I thought of myself and still claimed that I had low self-esteem. Yet I had to learn the hard way that this is where pride shows up the most, in those who think that they don't need help and those who think that without them the work, the job, the situation, the circumstance would never get better or changed. These kinds of people, myself included, ***pride themselves*** on working harder than anyone else. They overdo everything and they often over think everything as well.

Lesson number 2: Others bring their individuality to the puzzle (job, life, plans, or needs) and make it so much better. The bottom line is that we never see that we were actually milking our worth from the work. Performance, performance, performance was our life's blood. Even though we claimed that we had low self-worth, we gained value in the work we performed. It made us feel good to be needed and relied upon. Yet at the end of the workday, at the end of the assignment performed, we were already seeking the next assignment, on to the next day's work to obtain our daily dose of worth. This, too, is vain, and this, too, is pride.

To obtain your worth and value from anyone other than the God who made the heavens and the earth is worthless. This type of pride allows one to be dictated to, ruled by, and carried about solely on the whims of man and then to seek value in man's opinion alone.

Beloved, your worth and value in life and in death comes from the Lord. Have faith in that alone. Do not have faith in your ability to perform. This leads to pride and causes you to exalt your gift, talent, or skill over someone else. Often, we do it very subtly, and we may not recognize it. Perhaps those whom you are doing the work for don't recognize it, but you know who does recognize it: the Lord God Almighty. He sees, friend. He sees when you are walking in pride shrouded by good works.

When you seek the Lord for His truth regarding your worth, He will, over time, reveal His desire for you and increase your awareness regarding your performance and the reasons for you doing all that you do. In this, you begin to walk in a place of humility and sobriety, no longer being tipsy with others' approval of your performance. You walk solely in the pleasing eyes of your heavenly Father, knowing that your worth and value is wrapped up in Him and Him alone.

~Focus Point~

What good works have you done lately?

_____

_____

_____

_____

What "good" works have you done lately for the appeasing eyes of others watching?

_____

_____

_____

_____

Repent and ask your heavenly Father to reassign both your heart and hands so that the work that you do is for His glory from this day forward and reflects His heart and His heart alone.

_____

_____

_____

_____

Layer Eight ~ Day Six

Perfect Pride

Romans 12:16

"Be of the same mind toward one another. Do not set your mind on high things, but associate with the humble. Do not be wise in your own opinion."

~Heart Caption~

What does it mean to be of the same mind toward one another? With this story, I'll provide the answer. A consumer consultant formed a group of diverse individuals to determine the best way to meet the needs of a small community on the outskirts of town. In this group, there were a couple of doctors, lawyers, a few store clerks, two janitors, a single mom of 5 children, a homeless man, and a high school dropout. They were all placed in a large room with plenty of comfortable seating, table space, food, and beverages. They were asked to come up with the best plan within a two-hour span of time. After 15 minutes, the consumer consultant noticed from the viewing room that 3 groups had formed. The doctors and lawyers were group #1, the store clerks and janitors were group #2, and the single mom of 5, the homeless man, and the high school dropout made up group #3.

After one full hour had passed, the consultant re-entered the room and stood at the door, cleared his throat, and made his way to the podium. He began talking by thanking them for grouping themselves together in groups that allowed them to work effectively and efficiently together. Then he asked them, "What is your plan to meet the needs of the small community?" After everyone had ceased talking within their own groups, one representative was called to the podium to represent the entire group. However, when the lawyer began speaking, it was clear that his agenda was only for those in the community who were noted as the elite. The consumer consultant asked again for a representative for the entire group to come to the podium and state the proposed plan to meet the needs of the community. The store clerk stood up and walked to the podium, and she thanked everyone for coming and stated her plan to meet the needs of the community, which catered only to those in the community who were of the working class.

Lastly, the homeless man stood up and asked for permission to come to the podium. When he did, those in the previous two groups began to look away from him and were not paying attention when he began to speak. However, he brought up the fact that he had fallen on hard times after losing his wife and immediate family and then losing his job and home. He began to speak through tears of his former elaborate lifestyle and how his lifestyle had to change in order to help him understand the needs of the community. He began to look at everyone on the same level playing field in order to help everyone and not just a few. He said that the doctors and lawyers could orchestrate community involvement so that they are not the only ones benefitting from a house and a car, but so that the entire community is thriving. He continued by stating that the schools would be better if the community would help the single mother of 5 and the grocery store clerk did not have to remain in that position. There is room for growth for everyone, and the community would be made better, one life, one problem, and one success story at a time if they all joined together. The community would be better if no one thought themselves better than the other but they reached out to the entire community. It would indeed be a successful community and their strategy could be launched and even carried on in the next town, city, state, and region, if they all worked together.

Sometimes, it takes those who are humble to be an example to those who think higher of themselves than they should. For those of us who are believers, the Apostle Paul admonishes us to be of the same mind toward one another. That is where change happens: in us coming together, unifying our causes, connecting, and delivering a strategy to reach the community. When we all associate with the humble, we partake in all that God has in store for us. True humility is not thinking badly about yourself, but it is also not thinking less of others. True humility is esteeming God, His will, and His greatness in every area of our lives. This also is seeing the best in God's creation – humanity, who is made in His image. As believers, this creates a place where one truly is walking and journeying through life in humility, honoring the Lord, and being of one mind with his fellow man.

~Focus Point~

What are some ways that you can be of the same mind toward your family member or your neighbor?

_____

_____

_____

_____

What is your plan to exalt God in every area of the relationships noted above?

_____

_____

_____

_____

Layer Eight ~ Day Seven

Perfect Pride Poem

Everything I do has to be perfect. Everything I say has to be perfect.
That which my hands touch; the places where my feet go.
Everything I know has to be perfect.
Because it shows off me. It shows off the work of my hands.
It shows off my thoughts; it shows me.
Everything I do has to be perfect.
I didn't know how much work it took to be perfect.
It takes so much work; with everything I say, everything I do and put my hands to
I work so hard to make sure that everything is perfect.
When it comes tumbling down, when it's found out that everything is not perfect.
When it is seen and said that everything is not perfect – it's like the walls come tumbling down.
My perfect walls come tumbling down.
That's because God never made me to be perfect.
He never made me to display myself, my skills, the works of my hands, the works of my feet, the words of my mouth as perfect.
He never meant for this to display me as perfect.
I am made in His image; He humbled Himself and became obedient unto death.
The humility of Jesus gave my life salvation. He gave me a new heart. He gave me a new mind.
Now the words that I think and say are no longer my words.
It is for His wondrous glory that I yield my mind.

I yield my body, I yield – I give myself as an instrument of righteousness.
I yield myself as an instrument of praise. I yield my skill.
Everything no longer has to be perfect.
I no longer have to be perfect.
My perfection is giving God glory.
It's yielding to God's glory so that He is seen, He is magnified, He is exalted, He is praised and lifted high – not His creation but Him.
No longer I but Christ; He is exalted.

Layer Nine ~
Free Indeed

Layer Nine ~ Introduction

Free Indeed

God developed in me a love for the Word of God. He gave me a hunger and a thirst for His Word. I did not even recognize it as such, but I was so hungry for God! I was so hungry for what I now recognize as love, peace, and normalcy. God brought this into my life. I was able to see that in the Old Testament: the challenges, the difficulties, and the distraught home life that Hagar had; the disruption of Naomi and Ruth; and the challenges and mishandling of Tamar. I saw how God brought them out into their wealthy places. When everyone wrote them off and dismissed them in their difficulty, God stood for them, gave them a name in their story, and allowed those who would read their story to see His hands bringing deliverance to their lives.

Layer Nine ~ Day One

Free Indeed

Isaiah 61:1

"The Spirit of the Lord God is upon Me, Because the LORD has anointed Me To preach good tidings to the poor; He has sent Me to heal the brokenhearted, To proclaim liberty to the captives, And the opening of the prison to those who are bound."

~Heart Caption~

Throughout the pages of this devotional, the Lord God has been speaking and bringing good tidings to us on a daily basis. He has been illuminating our hearts through Scripture, heart captions, focus points, poems, participation, and even recommitting our lives back to the Father and renewing our relationship with Him in a fresh way. As we embark upon the last 7 days of this devotional, my only question left to ask is: "How badly do you want the deliverance Christ purchased with His life for you to receive?"

Friend, make no more excuses. You have lived life long enough and have made comments and excuses such as, "If it wasn't for this/that, I would give my life to Christ right now." "I still have more life to live, and I want to live it my way." "Well, the good Lord understands that I'm just not ready yet to go all in." Beloved, our next moments are not promised to us, and I simply want to remind you of what is available to you, what is waiting for you once you truly give your heart to the Lord God and receive the joyous salvation in Christ Jesus.

Christ has come for you because of His love for you. Did you know that? For every down day and every disappointed year you've experienced and desperately craved a way out, Christ was sent to you because of His love for you.

Do you have a broken heart? Have your dreams collapsed and died in the middle of them being fulfilled? Have you felt like quitting life because you felt there was no need to go on? Believer, do you have a broken heart, broken dreams, or a broken life? Christ was sent to you.

Is your heart being held captive to the yearnings and desires of this world and its culture? Friend, are you held captive by your past and unable to move forward into a future that God has planned for you? Do you desire to really be set free in your mind and body, once and for all? Christ was sent to you.

What has held you bound for so many years? You can see others getting free; you even desire to be free, but freedom always eludes you. Why, friend? Why aren't you free by now? You say you're happy and that you want to continue living your life just the way it is, but in the middle of the night, your heart and mind wander throughout the dry places looking and searching for refreshment. You are looking for change without the need to do anything differently. Friend, how long can you last like this? How long can your family last like this, bailing you out every time you get into some form of trouble? They've helped you until they themselves are bone dry, and some have even cut you off. When will you once and for all admit that enough is finally enough, friend?

Christ was sent for you. In order for all of these things to change in your life, you need to receive Him. No one is given a gift only to never receive it, open it up, and use, apply, or partake of the gift. Friend, it's now your turn. The call has gone out. The call went out in Isaiah 61:1 in the Old Testament, and 2,000 years ago the call went out again in Luke 4:18: *"The Spirit of the LORD is upon me, Because He has anointed Me To preach the gospel to the poor; He has sent Me to heal the brokenhearted, To proclaim liberty to the captives And recovery of sight to the blind, To set at liberty those who are oppressed."*

Luke's gospel goes on to say, *"Then He closed the book, and gave it back to the attendant and sat down. And the eyes of all who were in the synagogue were fixed on Him. And He began to say to them, 'Today this Scripture is fulfilled in your hearing'"* (Luke 4:20-21). Almost 2,000 years ago, this Scripture was fulfilled. Today, the Scriptures are still relevant and being fulfilled for those who will receive them. Will you receive what Christ was sent to give you? The question is now with you. As we continue in the final 6 days of this devotional, hear the Spirit of the living God calling out to you, encouraging you to know that freedom is simply YOURS for the asking.

~Focus Point~

As a place of testimony, make note and write down what the Lord has set you free from:

_____

_____

_____

_____

Christ was sent to you because of His love for you. Explain this statement as it applies to your life.

_____

_____

_____

_____

Layer Nine ~ Day Two

Free Indeed

John 8:32
"And you shall know the truth, and the truth shall make you free."

~Heart Caption~

After years of being an adult Christian and living my life alongside other Christians, I heard myself referred to as Ms. Super Christian. While I don't relish in this title, it was quite difficult and emotionally confusing to me to hear that this is how others saw me. I remember hearing one person that I really looked up to saying loudly, "You don't need to read 12 chapters of your Bible every day." I walked away from her and those who she was talking to, hurt and bewildered. Everyone wants to be someone's friend and viewed as a contributor to the friendship, not above the friendship. I had to learn that this was not the case in life.

Something I have discovered is that John 8:32 was realized in my life, simply by the hunger for the Word of God. Truthfully, I have always been a reader. I loved to not only collect books, magazines, and periodicals, but it was my practice to read each one and even to read them over again. This love for words written on paper increased in my life and in my spirit as I became a Christian. I would read the Word of God, and the Scriptures would simply pour over me like water in a desert. It was here that I discovered the truth of the Word of God, specifically John 8:32: *"and you shall know the truth, and the truth shall make you free."*

I have often heard it said in this manner, that it's the truth that you know that will make you free. Taking the latter impartation of this Scripture is what has driven me, and it is that which keeps, preserves, and centers me. I try to spend as much time in the Word of God as I can, especially because I understand that I will know the truth, and the truth shall make me and keep me free. Therefore, I gladly spend quality time in the Word of God.

There is wonderful revelation of this Scripture in the phrase *"you will know."* The Blue Letter Bible interprets this phrase as the Greek word *ginōskō,* which means to learn to know, to come to know, to get a knowledge of, perceive, feel, understand, or to become acquainted with. This phrase, according to the Blue Letter Bible, is also "a Jewish idiom for sexual intercourse between a man and a woman." What does this mean? This means that there is such a personal inner exchange that takes place when we read the Word of God wholeheartedly. We both receive and partake fully in the Word of God, and the application of the Word of God becomes the fruit of our interaction, our intercourse (contact, exchange) with and in the Scriptures. This is the level of reading that we must endeavor to have. It is this level of Scripture reading that results in a changed life, because it changes us forever for the good and for the glory of God.

Beloved, it is this type of Scripture reading that the Holy Spirit desires that we engage in. Let it be said that in hindsight, I am in full agreement now with the woman who said that we do not need to read 12 chapters of the Bible every day, if we are simply reading from the perspective of quantity only and not quality. It is life-changing to read the Bible from the perspective of reading one Scripture – memorizing and meditating on that one Scripture until your moment and your journey are permeated by that one Scripture. We must realize that we are not reading from the perspective of quantity but quality. For it is in this measure of Scripture receiving that we are changed.

Friend, it is this change that occurs, one Scripture at a time, one word at a time; we are changed, our hearts are renewed, and there is an impartation of Him to you and to me. Receive His Word anew, with fresh eyes and with an increased hunger, every time you come to it. This, friend, is the Word of God that sets us free, by the truth that we know.

~Focus Point~

Write out the Scripture verses that have impacted your life.

_____

_____

_____

_____

_____

_____

_____

_____

Due to these Scriptures listed above, list fruit that you have seen in your life as a result of the Word of God received, imparted, and practiced in your life.

_____

_____

_____

_____

Layer Nine ~ Day Three

Free Indeed

Galatians 5:1
"Stand fast therefore in the liberty by which Christ has made us free, and do not be entangled again with a yoke of bondage."

~Heart Caption~

How do you preach again to those who you've preached to before who have allowed themselves to get caught up in the same traps, the same dysfunctions and the same rebellion, the same bondage once again? I believe you simply remind them of the price Christ paid for their freedom. The price was high, and the sacrifice cost Him His life, and yet He made the choice to die so that you and I could be free. Now, with that freedom comes a responsibility to live free, walk free, talk free, and abide free in Christ. In order to remain free, you have to stand (persevere, persist) in or on something solid so that you may stand without wavering.

The Apostle Paul encourages us in Galatians to stand fast *in* the liberty (freedom from slavery, independence) by which Christ has made us free. Friend, we have been made free, we have been liberated for the purpose of freedom, and we have been chosen by God to no longer carry and not be ruled or judged by the oppressive requirements of the law. True joy is found in this fact; those of us who have placed our trust in Christ are free. We no longer follow the regimented regulations of laws that dictate a response, such as I have to do this to achieve that. Our relationship and hope is in Christ. Because we have a relationship with Him, out of the abundance of our heart, our relationship pours forth love and obedience to Him. We get to have fellowship with Him, and we get to draw near to the mercy seat. We get to enjoy His presence and come boldly to His throne so that we have the wonderful opportunity to obtain mercy and find help in our time of need (Hebrews 4:16).

The Apostle Paul provides a stern reminder: *"and do not be entangled **again** with a yoke of bondage."* Here is where the trouble takes shape. We often return to the same problem, somehow thinking within ourselves that we will do this but won't do that; I'll go here but I won't go there, I'll date him but I won't do that, I'll talk to her but I won't go home with her. In some form or fashion, we entangle ourselves with the very same yoke of bondage from which Christ is calling us away. This is the opportunity for us to stand fast, be persistent, and to persevere in the liberty by which Christ has made us free.

How does one stand fast? If you know that you have an appetite towards crack cocaine, make it your business to not dwell among and be friends with those who still sniff cocaine, smoke cocaine, or sell cocaine. If you have an appetite to drink alcohol, don't go to the liquor store to buy a Pepsi or a bag of chips. If you have an unsatiable appetite for sex, and you're still single (or married), don't sign up for dating websites and don't be too quick to go on dates, even with believers. Even though you are a confessing Christian, single, divorced, or widowed, you may not be ready to be in an atmosphere of dating just yet. Allow Christ to fully have access to your mind, heart, and all of your activities so that He can minister to you about who you should be in close proximity with regarding relationships, both female and male.

The Holy Spirit desires to be involved in every detail of your life, so intimately that He can guide you and direct you before things go wrong, rather than after things have gone wrong. When Christ is involved in your life daily, on a moment by moment basis, you should not find yourself in places that you shouldn't be, at least not by His leading. Remember, God is faithful, and even if things do go wrong and head in a different or wrong direction, the Holy Spirit is able to bring both you and your life back into alignment with His plans and purposes.

~Focus Point~

What are/were your yokes of bondage?

_____

_____

_____

_____

Write down areas of freedom over those yokes of bondage.

_____

_____

_____

_____

Take time and write your celebration and thank you to Christ for this freedom.

_____

_____

_____

_____

Layer Nine ~ Day Four

Free Indeed

Colossians 2:13

"And you, being dead in your trespasses and the uncircumcision of your flesh, He has made alive together with Him, having forgiven you all trespasses."

~Heart Caption~

For several years, I've looked for opportunities to share on the topic, "Are we dead yet?" You may recognize the familiarity of the topic from the movie titled, "Are We There Yet?" The movie centers around a family traveling for vacation, and as our children have done during drive-to vacations, their cry from the back seat was, "Are we there yet?" I've seen many people live out their lives as believers the same way they used to live as unbelievers, and I would often quietly say to myself and the Holy Spirit, "Are they dead yet?" This notion comes from the whole-hearted belief that if we are dead to something, whatever it is, we can no longer be aroused or affected either negatively or positively by the item, the attraction, or the temptation because we are dead to it and its effects.

Get this picture in your mind. Imagine a dead person in a coffin. As the mortician is preparing the body to be displayed during the wake and the funeral, the body is not reacting to what the mortician is doing. The mortician is dressing the body, applying appropriate makeup, and moving arms, hands, and feet, all in preparation for the displaying of the body during the ceremony of the wake and the funeral. The body does not rise up and say, "I am allergic to formaldehyde," nor does it say, "I don't like that shade of lipstick." The body also does not arise from death to say, "The tie is too tight and by the way, can I have a drink of water?" Nor does it say, "While you're smoking that cigarette, can I have a puff or two?"

The body is dead and has absolutely NO responses at all. The body and the senses that alerted him or her to that which used to tempt them while they were alive are now dead. The senses that used to alert him or her to lust are now dead. The senses that used to alert him or her to alcohol, cigarettes, lying, cheating, abusing their spouse, talking about their mother-in-law, hating their neighbor's children, or having sex are all now dead.

According to Colossians 2:13, we were dead in our trespasses and the uncircumcision of our flesh, but God made us alive together with Him, having forgiven all of our trespasses. He washed them clean from our soul. We no longer live in our former state of trespasses and uncircumcision. We are alive to Christ, raised to serve the living and true God. Romans 6:11 says, *"Likewise you also, reckon yourselves to be dead indeed to sin, but alive to God in Christ Jesus our Lord."* Continuing and living our lives to Christ, the Apostle Paul states in Romans 6:13, *"And do not present your members as instruments of unrighteousness to sin, but present yourselves to God as being alive from the dead, and your members as instruments of righteousness to God."*

Friend, in light of the Word of God which makes clear that we who are true believers in Christ and have accepted His sacrificial life to redeem us and make us a part of His Kingdom, the question still stands and makes even more sense now: Are we dead yet? If you are not dead indeed to sin, there is work on your part to do. This is the work of sanctification. Sanctification is being set apart for God for His use. However, this setting apart requires our direct participation. We have an active role to play; the work is not done unless we agree to the process and then participate in it. God works in us by His Holy Spirit to renew our minds and our hearts, which assist us in the

193

sanctification process. Through the Holy Spirit, we receive Christ as our Savior; as Jesus comes into our hearts, we are encouraged to read the Word of God to feed our spirit and communicate with our heavenly Father through prayer, and to be a part of a fellowship of other believers which brings about encouragement, fellowship and accountability. As our spirit is fed by the Word of God, we grow in both relationship with God and the people of God through fellowship.

Through our desire to please our heavenly Father and obey His Word, we lose the desire to do those things that we used to do; this may not happen overnight but over time. In some cases, people have experienced immediate deliverance from habits, while others have and may still be experiencing a process to their deliverance; each situation is unique to the person and their relationship with their heavenly Father. Each situation is unique to the *relationship* the believer has with their heavenly Father, not their religion or denomination. Remember, it is a relationship and your sanctification – being set apart for His divine purposes – will always extend from the root, the foundation of the relationship that you have with Him.

Layer Nine ~ Day Five

Free Indeed

Isaiah 64:6
"But we are all like an unclean thing,
And all our righteousnesses are like filthy rags;
We all fade as a leaf, And our iniquities, like the wind,
Have taken us away."

~Heart Caption~

The religious community is filled with people who do righteous works, such as giving to the poor and needy or doing good and not expecting anything in return. Righteous works are basically any or all forms of charity and benevolent giving in any way. Many do this benevolent or charity giving believing that they will be received into heaven for their works. However, Christians, those who are believers and have accepted the finished work of Christ for their sins, realize according to Isaiah 64:6, all of our righteousness is as filthy rags. None of our righteousness nor the righteousness of anyone on the planet will ever amount to Christ's sacrifice.

Christ saved us not because of righteous works we have done. We could never do enough nor pay enough, and for this I am tremendously thankful. For if salvation was something that we could do **works** for to enter into eternity, only the healthy would have eternal life. Those who are immobile, those who are paralyzed, or those who have any form of handicap would not receive eternal life. If eternal life was something that could be paid for, as the old saying goes, the rich would live eternally and the poor would die eternally. Christ's precious blood brought redemption for the world by His mercy. He provided the washing of regeneration and renewal by the Holy Spirit.

Beloved, it was through the mercy of Christ that He came to save us. We did nothing to earn it, and we did not deserve it. It was His love for us that caused Him to rise up and become the sacrificial Lamb needed to cleanse the earth by the washing of regeneration and bring about renewal by the Holy Spirit. This regeneration brings us out of our old ways by the rebirthing process of being born again. We are born again as new creations in Christ. Through the Holy Spirit and the Word of God, our hearts and minds are renewed, changed, and converted from the old way of thinking, the old way of talking, and the old way of living; we are born again. We look the same, but over time, we are noticeably different in our looks because the light of God comes upon us; we smile, and the joy of God's presence is now within us. We are now thriving and not merely existing. The life of God exists within us, and the newness of life and our regenerated existence are beaming forth. We are children of the Most High God, and we are beautifully renewed and regenerated in Him by His love. No works on our own could ever accomplish what Christ has finished on Calvary's cross. Forever settled in Heaven, His blood paid it all, and only to Him do we owe all.

~Focus Point~

Precious one, write your story of how you have been renewed by Christ's love:

_____

_____

_____

_____

196

Layer Nine ~ Day Six

Free Indeed

2 Corinthians 5:17
"Therefore, if anyone is in Christ, he is a new creation; old things have passed away; behold, all things have become new."

~Heart Caption~

I am new; He has made me new.
I am a new creation.
I see my life and my destiny with new eyes.
I see myself, not as the old but now as the new creation that He has promised I would be.
It took me some time to get here,
To the place of seeing me as He sees me.
New, a new creation.
The space in my life where the old has truly passed away;
the old that used to haunt me, run through my mind with thoughts that I would never be anything, I wasn't good enough for anything.
He, My Lord, My Faithful Keeper and Father, kept repeating to me, like a tape player continuously playing over in my head and my heart; you, daughter, you son, are My new creation.
Yes, I've created a beautiful universe;
I've created a wondrous earth,
But you, daughter or son I've made in My image, and I say to you: you are My new creation; your old has passed away.
Behold, your new has come; it is here.

Receive what I have died to give you.
For, I say to you, you are new.

Layer Nine ~ Day Seven

Free Indeed

John 8:36
"Therefore if the Son makes you free, you shall be free indeed."

~Heart Caption~

I remember laying in the middle of my mom's bed. It was the night of New Year's Eve more than 30 years ago, and I had just arrived home to my mom's house after one of the last crack binges I had been on. I lay in the middle of her bed, smelling her perfume, missing her, realizing all of the shame and embarrassment I had caused her, and feeling sorrowful for my inability to stop the crack binging. That night, my mom had left for church. She left and went to the house of God, which was her only help for her grown daughter whom she could not help. I stopped swirling in my defeat long enough to gather myself and go to the bathroom to take a shower. While in the shower, it felt as though God's liquid love poured over me; every inch of my being was showered, physically and emotionally, and covered by the felt presence of God's love.

I felt God calling my heart to Him. He was drawing me to Him with every drop of the shower's water, the cleansing of Holy Spirit, beating upon my body, the dripping of every drop of water. The Holy Spirit was calling me. While my mom was at church crying out for me, with every tear she shed, every tear that fell from her eyes and touched her cheeks, heaven's purifying waters were washing over me. The reassuring power of God caught up to the runner in me. The running, chasing, and never settling heart of mine was arrested by the Holy Spirit. The love of God poured out over me, and although I had a long way to go, God made it absolutely clear to me that I was on His radar screen.

When the Holy Spirit stepped forth into the beginning of my ending, He made it absolutely clear that the drawing, yearning, and chasing of crack cocaine in my mind and in my life were over. No power is stronger than the pull of the love of God, and when God says enough, it is enough. The surrender of my heart was imminent, and I welcomed the surrender of my heart to God. I was mentally, emotionally, and physically tired. I had no end in sight. I could not see my way through, but the Holy Spirit pulled me to the place in Him that finally made surrender complete.

One night in the shower changed my life and destiny forever. It began with feeling and experiencing the real love and presence of God being poured out upon my heart, my mind, and in my spirit. This was simply the beginning of God putting His finger on situations of my life and causing me to look at them through His eyes, allowing the change in my life to take place no matter how long it took. At least there was a beginning, and I was on my way.

This was the beginning of my process with the Lord by feeling Him, hearing Him, and believing in Him at a greater depth than what I had ever experienced before. What transpired from that experience was a realness of Him connecting to me in a tangible way that I had not felt before. My process was simply spending time in His presence that resulted in me no longer being able to find comfort in the sin that was luring me to hell. Everything I did from that point on continued to point me toward the deliverance that God was calling over my life. I no longer had pleasure in the sin that was overtaking my life. The Lord began to whisper and remind me of His love for me. Again and again I connected to this drawing; my heart connected, and I felt comfort, peace, safety, and finally surrender in the love of God.

When God set me free of crack cocaine, I have never returned to the drugs, the life of prostitution which the drugs drove me to, nor the demeaning lifestyles, the mental rejection of myself, or the self-shame that plagued my mind and heart after becoming addicted to drugs. Beloved, it was almost like I became invisible to the people who were hunting me down because they knew that all it took for me was just one drop of the drug and I was off on a tangent of smoking and doing everything at their beck and call. God even stopped that. Friend, there is a place in God where He places a shield and a protective covering over you, and you are no longer "visible" to your enemies. He brought finality to those who were chasing me, even though I didn't have enough sense to ask Him for this to be stopped in my life. His love surrounded me, shielded me, and protected me from the dangers of both the drugs and the people that I didn't even realize were hell-bent and sent by Satan himself to destroy my life.

Friend, allow the love of our heavenly Father to set you free from yourself. Allow the love of our heavenly Father to comfort, settle, and secure you in Him. No longer be driven by what you do, what you did, or who did what to you. Allow the love of our heavenly Father to pour over you, cleanse you, and purify you in His presence.

~Focus Point~

Write out your process or what you may remember of your process of the love of God drawing you.

_____

_____

_____

_____

_____

_____

_____

Where did the process of you experiencing the love of God draw you to?

_____

_____

_____

_____

If your process and experiencing the love of God places you in a place of surrender and thankfulness, write about it.

_____

_____

_____

_____

A Final Word

A Prostitute No Longer: The Devotional

It is my desire to be a voice to the hurting, the abused, and those who are struggling with choices. I was in the place of hurting, abuse, and my own struggles where I needed to hear a voice. Even in my disobedience, it would have been a light for me to hear a voice. In the darkness, a voice did rise up, and it was the voice of the Holy Spirit. In my rebellion, I rejected the only voice I knew, and after doing life on my own and by my own terms, I learned to listen to that voice. I learned to look to the gentle voice of my heavenly Father as He would speak to me through His Word, my pastor, and through other believers the Lord placed in my life.

However, the choice was mine. I had to learn to listen even when I didn't want to listen. Some folks learn to listen after they've received a sentence from the judge; others learn to listen while they're burying a loved one. Some choose not to listen, even while taking pills, drugs, and alcohol, cutting themselves, binging on sex or food only to spew out the food later. Unfortunately, they and others have convinced themselves that there is no way out. But there is always a voice.

Precious friend, the Lord desires to speak with you, and through His love and mercy, He will bring you out of the situation you are in. It may be a heavy load to lift, but I promise you the Lord can lift you out of any situation or circumstance you find yourself in. It may not be an immediate release, but stay close to Him. Sometimes, the process can be the most wearisome so that we avoid it altogether. Listen, precious one; the process is where pain is released and healing is provided, but you have to go through it. Go through your process wherever you need to.

The Lord, our heavenly Father, is waiting on you for your yes. The moment that you turn your face to Him, you will find that He is there. He will prove to be good for you all the days of your life. Lean into Him and not another. All others on planet earth have to pass through the shadow of death. Wouldn't you want to be with someone who has already taken the trip and have come out triumphantly? Christ has! If you have a situation that looks like death to you, He can get you through. Turn your face to Him. I promise you that He'll do you good all the days of your life.

Index

Layer Two	**Father to the Fatherless**
Day One	*Psalm 68:5 "**A Father of the fatherless**, a defender of widows, is God in His holy habitation."*
Day Two	*Psalm 68:5 "A Father of the fatherless, **a defender of widows**, is God in His holy habitation."*
Day Three	*Isaiah 64:8 "But now, O LORD, **You are our Father**; We are the clay, and You our potter; And all we are the work of your hand."*
Day Four	*2 Corinthians 6:18 "**I will be a Father to you**, And you shall be My sons and daughters, Says the LORD Almighty."*
Day Five	*Psalm 103:13 (NLT) "**The LORD is like a father to his children**, tender and compassionate to those who fear him."*
Day Six	*John 1:12-13 "But as many as received Him, to them He gave the right to become children of God, to those who believe in His name: who were born, not of blood, nor of the will of the flesh, nor of the will of man, but of God."*
Day Seven	*Psalm 27:10 "When my father and my mother forsake me, Then the LORD will take care of me."*

Layer Three	**Delayed Growth**
Day One	*1 Peter 2:2 "As newborn babes, **desire the pure milk of the word**, that you may grow thereby."*

Day Two   *2 Peter 1:5-8 "But also for this very reason, **giving all diligence, add to your faith virtue, to virtue knowledge**, to knowledge self-control, to self-control perseverance, to perseverance godliness, to godliness brotherly kindness, and to brotherly kindness love. For if these things are yours and abound, you will be neither barren nor unfruitful in the knowledge of our Lord Jesus Christ."*

Day Three   *2 Peter 1:5-8 "But also for this very reason, giving all diligence, add to your faith virtue, to virtue knowledge, **to knowledge self-control, to self-control perseverance**, to perseverance godliness, to godliness brotherly kindness, and to brotherly kindness love. For if these things are yours and abound, you will be neither barren nor unfruitful in the knowledge of our Lord Jesus Christ."*

Day Four   *2 Peter 1:5-8 "But also for this very reason, giving all diligence, add to your faith virtue, to virtue knowledge, to knowledge self-control, to self-control perseverance, **to perseverance godliness, to godliness brotherly kindness, and to brotherly kindness love**. For if these things are yours and abound, you will be neither barren nor unfruitful in the knowledge of our Lord Jesus Christ."*

Day Five   *2 Peter 1:5-8 "But also for this very reason, giving all diligence, add to your faith virtue, to virtue knowledge, to knowledge self-control, to self-control perseverance, to perseverance godliness, to godliness brotherly kindness, and to brotherly kindness love. **For if these things are yours and abound**, you will be neither barren nor unfruitful in the knowledge of our Lord Jesus Christ."*

Day Six	*2 Peter 1:5-8 "But also for this very reason, giving all diligence, add to your faith virtue, to virtue knowledge, to knowledge self-control, to self-control perseverance, to perseverance godliness, to godliness brotherly kindness, and to brotherly kindness love. For if these things are yours and abound, **you will be neither barren nor unfruitful** in the knowledge of our Lord Jesus Christ."*
Day Seven	*2 Peter 1:5-8 "But also for this very reason, giving all diligence, add to your faith virtue, to virtue knowledge, to knowledge self-control, to self-control perseverance, to perseverance godliness, to godliness brotherly kindness, and to brotherly kindness love. For if these things are yours and abound, you will be neither barren nor unfruitful **in the knowledge of our Lord Jesus Christ."***

Layer Four   Unhealthy Exposure

Day One	*Psalm 54:1 "Save me, O God, by Your name, and vindicate me by Your strength."*
Day Two	*Psalm 54:2 "Hear my prayer, O God; give ear to the words of my mouth."*
Day Three	*Psalm 54:3 "For strangers have risen up against me, and oppressors have sought after my life; they have not set God before them. Selah."*
Day Four	*Psalm 54:4 "Behold, God is my helper; the Lord is with those who uphold my life."*
Day Five	*Psalm 54:5 "He will repay my enemies for their evil. Cut them off in Your truth."*
Day Six	*Psalm 54:6 "I will freely sacrifice to You; I will praise Your name, O LORD, for it is good."*

210

Day Seven *Psalm 54:7 "For He has delivered me out of all trouble; And my eye has seen its desire upon my enemies."*

Layer Five   Self Esteem

Day One *Ephesians 2:10 "For we are His workmanship, created in Christ Jesus for good works, which God prepared beforehand that we should walk in them."*

Day Two *Psalm 139:14 "I will praise You, for I am fearfully and wonderfully made; Marvelous are Your works, and that my soul knows very well."*

Day Three *Song of Solomon 4:7 "You are all fair, my love, And there is no spot in you."*

Day Four *Psalm 139:16 "Your eyes saw my substance, being yet unformed. And in Your book they all were written, the days fashioned for me, When as yet there were none of them."*

Day Five *Judges 6:14-15 "Then the LORD turned to him and said, 'Go in this might of yours, and you shall save Israel from the hand of the Midianites. Have I not sent you?' So he said to Him, 'O my Lord, how can I save Israel? Indeed my clan is the weakest in Manasseh, and I am the least in my father's house.'"*

Day Six *Romans 12:3 "For I say, through the grace given to me, to everyone who is among you, not to think of himself more highly than he ought to think, but to think soberly, as God has dealt to each one a measure of faith."*

Day Seven *Zephaniah 3:17 "The LORD your God in your midst, The Mighty One, will save; He will rejoice over you with gladness, He will quiet you with His love, He will rejoice over you with singing."*

Layer Six   Shame, Rejection, and Guilt

Day One   *Isaiah 61:7 "Instead of your shame you shall have double honor, And instead of confusion they shall rejoice in their portion. Therefore in their land they shall possess double; Everlasting joy shall be theirs."*

Day Two   *Matthew 26:31-35 "Then Jesus said to them, 'All of you will be made to stumble because of Me this night, for it is written:*

'I will strike the Shepherd,
And the sheep of the flock will be scattered.'

But after I have been raised, I will go before you to Galilee.'

Peter answered and said to Him, 'Even if all are made to stumble because of You, I will never be made to stumble.'

Jesus said to him, 'Assuredly, I say to you that this night, before the rooster crows, you will deny Me three times.'

Peter said to Him, 'Even if I have to die with You, I will not deny You!'

And so said all the disciples."

Day Three *Isaiah 49:15 "Can a woman forget her nursing child, And not have compassion on the son of her womb? Surely they may forget, Yet I will not forget you."*

Day Four   *Isaiah 49:16 "See, I have inscribed you on the palms of My hands; Your walls are continually before Me."*

Day Five   *Hebrews 13:5 "Let your conduct be without covetousness; be content with such things as you have. For He Himself has said, 'I will never leave you nor forsake you.'"*

Day Six   *Colossians 2:11-15 "In Him you were also circumcised with the circumcision made without hands, by putting off the body of the sins of the flesh,*

by the circumcision of Christ, buried with Him in
baptism, in which you also were raised
with Him through faith in the working of God, who
raised Him from the dead. And you, being dead in
your trespasses and the uncircumcision of your flesh,
He has made alive together with Him, having
forgiven you all trespasses, having wiped out
the handwriting of requirements that was against us,
which was contrary to us. And He has taken it out of
the way, having nailed it to the cross. Having
disarmed principalities and powers, He made a
public spectacle of them, triumphing over them in it."

Day Seven *Romans 8:1 "There is therefore now no condemnation*
to those who are in Christ Jesus, who do not walk
according to the flesh, but according to the Spirit."

Layer Seven Fear

Day One *Genesis 3:9-10 "Then the LORD God called to Adam*
and said to him, 'Where are you?' So he said, 'I heard
Your voice in the garden, and I was afraid because I
was naked; and I hid myself.'"

Day Two *1 John 4:18 "There is no fear in love; but perfect love*
casts out fear, because fear involves torment. But he
who fears has not been made perfect in love."

Day Three *Psalm 56:3-4 "Whenever I am afraid, I will trust in*
You. In God (I will praise His word), In God I have put
my trust; I will not fear. What can flesh do to me?"

Day Four *Deuteronomy 31:6 "Be strong and of good courage,*
do not fear nor be afraid of them; for the LORD your
God, He is the One who goes with you. He will not
leave you nor forsake you."

Day Five	*Psalm 27:1 "The LORD is my light and my salvation; whom shall I fear? The LORD is the strength of my life; Of whom shall I be afraid?"*
Day Six	*Isaiah 41:13 "For I, the LORD your God, will hold your right hand, saying to you, 'Fear not, I will help you.'"*
Day Seven	*Mark 5:36 "As soon as Jesus heard the word that was spoken, He said to the ruler of the synagogue, 'Do not be afraid; only believe.'"*

Layer Eight   Perfect Pride

Day One	*1 Corinthians 13:4 "Love suffers long and is kind; love does not envy; love does not parade itself, is not puffed up."*
Day Two	*1 Peter 5:5 "Likewise you younger people, submit yourselves to your elders. Yes, all of you be submissive to one another, and be clothed with humility, for 'God resists the proud, But gives grace to the humble.'"*
Day Three	*1 Peter 5:6 "Therefore humble yourselves under the mighty hand of God, that He may exalt you in due time."*
Day Four	*Proverbs 22:4 "By humility and the fear of the LORD Are riches, honor, and life."*
Day Five	*Romans 12:3 "For I say, through the grace given to me, to everyone who is among you, not to think of himself more highly than he ought to think, but to think soberly, as God has dealt to each one a measure of faith."*
Day Six	*Romans 12:16 "Be of the same mind toward one another. Do not set your mind on high things, but associate with the humble. Do not be wise in your own opinion."*

Layer Nine   Free Indeed

Day One   *Isaiah 61:1 "The Spirit of the Lord GOD is upon Me, Because the LORD has anointed Me To preach good tidings to the poor; He has sent Me to heal the brokenhearted, To proclaim liberty to the captives, And the opening of the prison to those who are bound."*

Day Two   *John 8:32 "And you shall know the truth, and the truth shall make you free."*

Day Three   *Galatians 5:1 "Stand fast therefore in the liberty by which Christ has made us free, and do not be entangled again with a yoke of bondage."*

Day Four   *Colossians 2:13 "And you, being dead in your trespasses and the uncircumcision of your flesh, He has made alive together with Him, having forgiven you all trespasses."*

Day Five   *Isaiah 64:6 "But we are all like an unclean thing, And all our righteousnesses are like filthy rags; We all fade as a leaf, And our iniquities, like the wind, Have taken us away."*

Day Six   *2 Corinthians 5:17 "Therefore, if anyone is in Christ, he is a new creation; old things have passed away; behold, all things have become new."*

Day Seven   *John 8:36 "Therefore if the Son makes you free, you shall be free indeed."*

Made in the USA
Middletown, DE
25 February 2022

61822377R00126